JAMESTOWN

Heritage

READERS

Book E

Lee Mountain, Ed.D.
University of Houston, Texas

Sharon Crawley, Ed.D.
Florida Atlantic University

Edward Fry, Ph.D.
Professor Emeritus
Rutgers University

Jamestown Publishers
Providence, Rhode Island

Favorite Children's Classics

ILLUSTRATED BY THE BEST ARTISTS
FROM THE PAST AND PRESENT

Jamestown Heritage Readers, Book E
Catalog No. 955
Catalog No. 955H, Hardcover Edition

© 1991 by Jamestown Publishers, Inc.

Cover and text design by Deborah Hulsey Christie
Cover and border illustrations by Pamela R. Levy

Printed in the United States of America

2   3   4   5   6   HA   96   95   94   93

ISBN 0-89061-955-7
ISBN 0-89061-714-7, Hardcover Edition

C·O·N·T·E·N·T·S

ONE
Tales Retold

TWO

Here and There, Then and Now

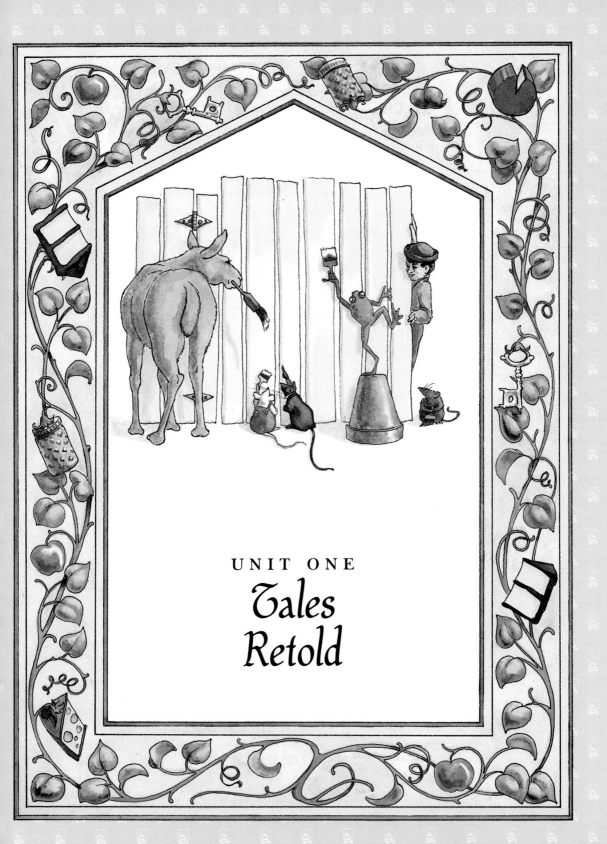

UNIT ONE

Tales
Retold

The Glorious Whitewasher

from

THE ADVENTURES OF TOM SAWYER

by

MARK TWAIN

om!"

No answer.

"Tom Sawyer!"

No answer.

"What's wrong with that boy, I wonder? You, TOM!"

No answer.

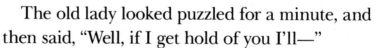

The old lady looked puzzled for a minute, and then said, "Well, if I get hold of you I'll—"

She did not finish, for by this time she was bending down and punching under the bed with the broom, so she needed breath for the punches. She brought forth nothing but the cat.

"I never did see the beat of that boy!"

She went to the open door and stood in it and looked out into the garden. No Tom. So she lifted up her voice and shouted, "Y-o-u-u, Tom!"

There was a slight noise behind her.

She turned just in time to grab a small boy.

"There! I might have thought of the kitchen closet. What you been doing in there?"

"Nothing."

"Nothing! Look at your hands, and look at your mouth. What is that?"

"I don't know, aunt."

"Well, I know. It's jam, that's what it is. Ten times I've said if you didn't let that jam alone I'd beat you."

"My! Look behind you, aunt!"

She wheeled around and grabbed up her skirts. The boy dashed out of her reach. In a flash, he was up the high board fence, over it, and out of sight.

His Aunt Polly stood surprised for a second. Then she broke into a laugh.

"Hang the boy! Can't I never learn anything? Ain't he played me tricks enough like that for me to be looking out for him by this time? But old fools are the biggest fools there is. Can't teach an old dog new tricks, as the saying is. That boy knows if he can make me laugh, I can't hit him.

"Well, I ain't doing right by that boy if I don't get after him. He's just too full of tricks, always headin' for trouble. But he's my own dead sister's boy, poor thing, and somehow I ain't got the heart to beat him the way I should.

11

"Every time I let him off, I know I'm doing wrong by him. But every time I hit him, my old heart most breaks. Well, I'll make him work tomorrow. It's mighty hard to make him work Saturdays while all the boys are playing. But he hates work more than he hates anything else, and I've got to do right by that child."

Saturday morning came. All the world was bright and fresh and full of life. There was a song in every heart. There was cheer in every face and a spring in every step.

Tom came out on the sidewalk with a pail of whitewash and a paint brush. He looked at the fence. All joy left him. The fence ran the whole way across the front yard, and it was nine feet high. Sighing, he wet his brush and passed it over the first board. He did it again and again.

Then Tom stood back and looked at his work. There were only a few whitewashed boards. There was still a far-reaching stretch of fence that was not yet whitewashed. Sighing, he sat down on a box.

Tom began to think of the good times he had planned for this day. Soon all the boys would come tripping along, and they'd make a world of fun of him for having to work. The very thought of it burned him like fire.

THREE
The Whole Chapter

FOUR
Numbers, Nature, and Nonsense

At this dark time, an idea flashed into his mind—a great idea, an idea that just might work.

With a smile on his face, Tom took up his brush and started whitewashing the fence.

Ben Rogers came into sight. He was eating an apple and giving forth deep-voiced orders, for he was pretending to be a boat captain on the river. "Stop her, sir! Ship up to back!" He held his arms straight at his sides. "Set her back. Stop her. Get out that line. Quick, now!"

Tom went on whitewashing. He didn't even give a look to the boat captain.

Ben stared a minute and then said, "Hi!"

No answer. Tom looked at his last touch with the eye of an artist. Then he gave a second coating of whitewash to a board he had finished and stood back to look again.

Ben came up beside him.

Tom's mouth watered for Ben's apple, but he stuck to his work.

"You got to work, hey?" said Ben.

Tom wheeled suddenly and said, "Why, it's you, Ben. I wasn't noticing."

"Say, I'm going in swimming, I am. Don't you wish you could? But of course you'd have more fun working, wouldn't you? Course you would!"

13

Tom stared at the boy a bit. Then he said, "What do you call work?"

"Why, ain't that work?" asked Ben.

Tom went back to his whitewashing. "Well, maybe it is, and maybe it ain't. All I know is, it suits Tom Sawyer."

"Oh come, now. You don't mean to let on that you like it?"

The brush kept on moving.

"Like it? Well, I don't see why I shouldn't like it. Does a boy get a chance to whitewash a fence every day?"

That put the thing in a new light. Ben stopped eating his apple. Tom worked his brush back and forth. He stepped back for a look. Then he added a touch here and there. Ben watched every move and got more and more interested.

At last he said, "Say, Tom, let me whitewash a little."

Tom thought it over, was about to say yes, but then changed his mind. "No, it wouldn't hardly do, Ben. You see, Aunt Polly's mighty picky about how this fence looks. It's right here on the street, you know. If it was the back fence, I wouldn't mind and she wouldn't, but she's mighty picky about this front fence. It's got to be done very careful. I suppose

Collection of the William A. Farnsworth Library and Art Museum

15

there ain't one boy in a hundred, maybe two hundred, that can do it the way it's got to be done."

"No, is that so? Oh come, now, let me just try, only just a little. I'd let you, if you was me, Tom," Ben said coaxingly.

"Ben, I'd like to, I would. But Aunt Polly—well, if you was to go at this fence, and anything was to happen to it—"

"Oh, come on, I'll be just as careful. Now let me try. Say, I'll give you a bite of my apple."

"Well, here—No, Ben, now don't. I'm afraid—"

"I'll give you all of my apple."

Tom gave up the brush with worry on his face, but joy in his heart. While Ben worked in the hot sun, Tom sat close by under a tree. As he ate Ben's apple, he planned how he could pull the same trick on some other friends.

Boys happened along every little while. They came to laugh and make fun, but they stayed to whitewash. By the time Ben was tired, Tom had given the next turn to Billy Fisher for a kite. When Billy Fisher was played out, Johnny Miller bought in for a dead rat and a string to swing it with, and so on, and so on, hour after hour.

By the time the middle of the afternoon came, Tom was rich. Besides the kite and the rat, he had a piece of blue bottle glass to look through, a key, a rope with a knot in it that nobody could untie, a silver dog tag—but no dog—and four pieces of orange.

He had had a nice time, laying about, all the while. Lots of talk with friends, and the fence had three coats of whitewash on it! If he hadn't run out of whitewash, he could have cleaned out the pockets of every boy in the village.

Tom said to himself that it was not such a bad world, after all. He had learned a great truth, without knowing it—that in order to make someone want a thing, you have to make the thing hard to get. He understood that work is whatever a body *has* to do, and play is whatever a body does not have to do.

The boy thought over these ideas for a while. Then he went to tell his Aunt Polly that the fence was done.

◆ ◆ ◆ ◆

Why are people still retelling the story of Tom and the whitewashed fence more than a hundred years after Mark Twain wrote his books about Tom Sawyer? Maybe it's because the idea behind Tom's trick still works. And maybe it's because boys and girls today are still thinking about the ideas that Tom thought about at the end of the story.

Amy's Trouble at School

from

LITTLE WOMEN

by

LOUISA MAY ALCOTT

Little Women is a book about four sisters—Meg, Jo, Beth, and Amy March. Amy is the youngest, and she is being teased by her older sister Jo as this part of the story begins.

my stood at the window and watched the boy next door ride by on horseback. She waved to him. "Our neighbor is quite a Cyclops, isn't he?" she said.

Her big sister Jo looked down at her. "What a thing to say about him! He's got both his eyes!"

"I didn't say anything about his eyes," said Amy. "I really don't see why you're getting angry just because I was saying how well he rides that horse."

"Oh, you silly goose!" exclaimed Jo, laughing. "You meant a centaur—half man, half horse—and you called him a Cyclops. That's a giant with one eye, Amy."

"You needn't laugh at me," sniffed Amy. "I don't need to be given a hard time at home. I'm having enough trouble at school these days."

"What do you mean?" asked Jo, more kindly, for Amy did sound as if her feelings were hurt. "What kind of trouble are you having at school?"

"It's all because of pickled limes," Amy started. "The other girls are always buying them, and if you don't want to be talked about, you must do it, too."

"Pickled limes? Are they the thing now? It used to be rock candy when I was at your school." Jo tried to keep from smiling, since Amy looked so worried.

"It's nothing but limes now," said Amy. "If one girl likes another, she gives her a lime. If she's mad at her, she eats one before her face and doesn't share. I've had ever so many, but I haven't returned them, and I should, for everyone is talking about me, I'm afraid."

Jo dug into her pocketbook. "Here," she said, handing all her change to Amy. "Make it last as long as you can."

"Oh, thank you," said Amy. "I'm going right to the store. I haven't had a lime this week. You see, I didn't want to take any more from my friends, since I couldn't return them. I can hardly wait to taste one again."

The next day, Amy was a bit late to school. She wanted to have all eyes upon her as she walked into Mr. Davis's classroom. She carried an interesting brown bag to her desk.

There was a lot of whispering in the next few minutes. The story traveled quickly from girl to girl. Soon everyone knew that Amy March had a bag of pickled limes with her and was going to share them.

At once the attention of her friends became marked. Katy Brown invited her to her next party on the spot. May Kingsley said that Amy could wear her new ring until lunch.

Jenny Snow, who had laughed at Amy's limeless state, tried to make up by passing over the answers to some homework questions, but Amy had not forgotten Jenny Snow's cutting words. Jenny had made jokes about "people whose noses were too stuck-up to notice other people's limes." So Amy put down Jenny's hopes right away. She passed Jenny a note saying, "You needn't be so nice all of a sudden, for you won't get any."

Jenny read the note. She gave Amy a look that said, "You'll be sorry," but Amy paid no attention.

A few minutes later, Jenny walked up to the teacher's desk. She acted as if she were just asking Mr. Davis a question, but in a low whisper, she told Mr. Davis that Amy March had a bag of pickled limes in her desk.

Now Mr. Davis had said the week before that there were to be no more limes brought to class. He had promised that the next girl found with limes would be a sad and sorry young lady. So, at the word *limes,* he turned red in the face and banged on his desk with his ruler.

Jenny slipped back into her seat in a hurry.

"Class, attention, if you please," ordered Mr. Davis.

All talking stopped. All pairs of blue, black, gray, and brown eyes were fixed upon him.

"Amy March, come to my desk."

Amy started to get to her feet. She tried to smile, but a secret fear was growing within her.

"Bring with you the limes you have in your desk." Those words stopped Amy before she got out of her seat.

"Don't take all," whispered the girl who sat by her.

Quickly, Amy shook out a few from the top of the bag. She carried the rest up to Mr. Davis's desk and laid them down before him. Maybe, she hoped, maybe he would be easy on her. Maybe he would even let her keep the limes. How could he stay cross when their wonderful smell met his nose?

But Mr. Davis hated the smell of pickled limes.

"Is that all of them?" he asked.

"Not quite," Amy answered in a very low tone.

"Bring the rest at once," he ordered.

With a deep sigh, Amy did as she was told.

"You are sure there are no more?"

"I never lie, sir."

"So I see," said Mr. Davis. "Now take the limes, two by two, and throw them into the garbage can."

Red with shame, Amy went back and forth time and again. Her friends sighed each time a pair of limes fell from her hands.

As Amy returned from her last trip, Mr. Davis

said, "I am sorry this has happened, but you must learn not to break my rules." He lifted his ruler. "Hold out your hand."

Amy jumped back and put both hands behind her.

"Your hand!" ordered Mr. Davis.

Too proud to cry, Amy set her teeth, threw back her head, and held out her hand.

The blows were neither many nor heavy, but that made no difference to Amy. For the first time in her life, she had been hit with a ruler, and in her eyes the shame was as great as if he had knocked her down.

"You will now stand in the corner until lunch," Mr. Davis went on.

That was terrible. It would have been bad enough to go to her seat and see the sad faces of her friends and the pleased faces of her enemies, but to stand until lunch, facing the whole class with the shame fresh upon her, seemed too much. For a second, she felt she could only drop down where she stood and cry.

But the thought of Jenny Snow kept her from breaking down and letting everyone know how terrible she felt. She fixed her eyes on a spot on the wall above what now seemed a sea of faces, and she stood there, so still and white that the class found it very hard to study for the rest of the morning.

The Lama

by

OGDEN NASH

The one-l lama,
He's a priest.
The two-l llama,
He's a beast.

And I will bet
A silk pajama
There isn't any
Three-l lllama.*

*There is, however, that huge type of fire
which firefighters call a "three-alarmer."

25

Vowel Riddle

by

JONATHAN SWIFT

We are very little creatures,
All of different voice and features.
One of us in *glass* is set.
One of us you'll find in *jet.*
Another you may see in *tin.*
And the fourth a *box* within.
If the fifth you should pursue,
It can never fly from *you.*

One Guess

by

ROBERT FROST

He has dust in his eyes and a fan for a wing,
A leg akimbo with which he can sing,
And a mouthful of dye stuff instead of a sting.

Robinson Crusoe on the Island

from ROBINSON CRUSOE

by DANIEL DEFOE

I, Robinson Crusoe, did not think I would live through so terrible a storm at sea. It started on September 30, 1659. All day our ship rocked far to one side, then to the other.

Toward evening a huge wave, mountain-like, came rolling toward our ship. It broke over us with a crash, and down came our sails!

We were in sight of land, but the shore looked rocky. The wild winds had driven our ship so far off course that we had no idea what land we were near.

I was hanging to the railing when the ship hit a rock. In that wild water we could not hope to have the ship hold together many minutes without breaking into pieces. The men called from below that she was already taking in water.

At once, we put down a little boat over the ship's side, and all getting into it, we braved the wild sea.

The wind drove us toward the land, but it did not look inviting. Then a giant wave rolled over us. It upset the boat, throwing us into the water. We were all swallowed up that second.

Nothing can tell how I felt when I sank in the water. Though I swam well, I could not get above water to draw a breath. That wave drove me and carried me a good way toward the land, and having spent itself, it rolled back and left me able to touch bottom.

I tried to get to my feet and walk forward before another wave would return and take me up again. But I could not move fast enough. I saw the sea come after me as high as a great hill, and as angry as an enemy. So I tried to hold my breath, and raise myself upon the water, if I could.

The wave that came upon me buried me at once twenty or thirty feet deep in its own body. I could feel myself carried a great way. I held my breath and tried to swim forward with all my might.

I was ready to burst with holding my breath when I felt myself coming up. My head shot out above the water. Though I could keep myself up for only two or three seconds, those seconds gave me the air I needed.

When the water began to return, I felt ground again with my feet. Then I ran with what strength I had onto the land. There I climbed up on a little hill where I was out of the reach of the water.

When I caught my breath, I walked about, looking for my friends, but there did not seem to be one person saved but myself. The sea buried all the rest.

Night was coming upon me. I moaned and held my head, certain that wild animals would come out in the dark. They would kill me and eat me.

My only hope, I thought, was to climb high into a tree. There I would place myself so that if I should sleep, I would not fall. I found a large bushy tree nearby, and I climbed.

Feeling more tired than ever before in my life, I slept soundly, though it rained and stormed all night.

In the morning I saw to my surprise that my ship, which had been caught on the rocks, was not broken to pieces. She lay, as the wind and sea had tossed her, up on the land, about two miles on my right.

I walked as far as I could toward her. But I found a wide neck of water between me and the ship, so I pulled off my shirt and started swimming.

When I came to the ship, I wondered how to get on board. As she lay grounded and high out of the water, there was nothing within my reach to lay hold of. I swam around her and spotted a small piece of rope hanging over the side. With much trouble I got hold of it, and by the help of that rope I climbed up and got on board.

First I went to the bread room. The food was dry. Being very hungry, I filled my pockets with bread.

I ate it as I went about other things, for I had no time to lose. From the wood on board, I needed to build a raft.

It was a small raft, so I had to think carefully of what was most important to take back with me right away. I decided on a box of bread, rice, cheeses, and dried meat.

While I was doing this, the tide began to wash out to sea. As I looked back across the neck of water, I saw my shirt, which I had left on the sand, swim away.

This set me hunting for clothes, of which I found enough, but I took no more than I needed for present use.

I had other things in mind, for which I had greater need. First, tools for building. I found a box of tools, which was indeed a prize to me, better than gold at that time.

My next care was for a gun for hunting, and I had to have some small bags of shot.

Then I boarded my raft. The wind was not strong, but it was enough to blow me toward the land.

I must not forget that we had on board the ship a dog and two cats. I carried both cats with me. As for the dog, he jumped off the ship by himself, and he swam to shore.

That dog was my good friend for many years. I wanted for nothing that he could bring me. I only wished he could talk to me, but that he could not do.

For most of October, I went back and forth to the ship again and again, bringing all I could to my island. But near the end of the month, it blew very hard one night. In the morning when I looked out, there was no more ship to be seen.

I was surprised. But mainly I felt glad that I had lost no time and had gotten everything out of her that I could use. Indeed, there was little left on that ship that I could have brought away, had I had more time.

Every day I went out with my gun to hunt for food. One time I killed a she-goat, and her kid followed me home. Another time I shot a large bird which was very good to eat, but I know not what to call it.

Soon I began to order my times of work, of going out with my gun, and time of sleep. Each morning I hunted for two or three hours, if it did not rain. Then I ate what I had to live on. From noon to two I lay down in my tent to sleep, the weather being very hot. Then in the evening I would work again.

The working parts of my day were used in making a table. I was as yet a very sorry workman, but time and need made me very good soon after, as I believe it would do for anyone else.

I longed for candles, for as soon as it was dark, I had to go to bed. But I had no candles from the ship. The best I could do was to save the fat whenever I killed a goat. I put the fat in a little dish made of clay, which I baked in the sun.

To this I added a wick of string. This gave me some light, though not the clear light of a real candle, but it let me work a bit after dark.

For many days I had been digging behind my tent into the rock, to make a little cave-like room to store my food and tools. The idea came to me that I should make this cave big enough to live in. My tent would not last through many more rain storms.

It took me seven months to dig out my cave-home.

One day, as I was busy inside my cave, I was terribly frightened with a most surprising thing indeed, for on a sudden, two of the posts I had put up in the cave cracked. I found the earth dropping down from the roof of my cave over my head. The top of my cave was falling in. For fear I should be buried in it, I ran outside.

I had no sooner stepped out than I knew my island was in the middle of a terrible earthquake. The ground I stood on shook three times. A great piece of the rock near me fell down with as loud a noise as I ever heard in all my life.

The sea came alive with waves higher than buildings. The earthquake must have been even stronger under the water than on the island.

The shaking of the ground upset my stomach.

I was so surprised with the thing itself, having never been in an earthquake before, or talked with anyone who had, that I was like someone in a dream. But the noise of the falling rocks woke me up, as it were.

I sank to the ground, sick with fear. I could think of nothing but the hill falling upon my tent, and all my goods, and burying all at once. Maybe I would be safer farther away from the rocky hill, but everything I had worked on was there.

The wind was still wild, but I felt no more shaking of the ground for some time. Still, I could not bring myself to go back in my cave for fear of being buried alive, so I sat upon the ground, not knowing what to do.

The downpour of rain kept me as wet as if I were swimming. The wind picked up strength. The sea was covered over with white caps. The wind rose higher and roared through the trees as if it were trying to tear them up by their roots.

I was near to being blown away in the storm that followed the earthquake, so I had to go back into my cave. But I was very much afraid it would fall on my head.

The fear of being swallowed up alive would not let me sleep, but by morning my eyes were so heavy that I dropped off for a few hours.

I Stood Like One Thunderstruck. N. C. Wyeth, 1920

As soon as I woke up, I decided that if this island had earthquakes, there would be no living for me in a cave. I must build a little place for myself in an open space, or I was certain at one time or another to be buried alive.

•   •   •   •

Robinson Crusoe later found out that he was not alone on the island. More than one reader has said that his or her heart missed a beat when Robinson Crusoe came upon a footprint in the sand. If you want to find out about that famous footprint, read the book *Robinson Crusoe.*

Proverbs

from

POOR RICHARD'S ALMANACK

by

BENJAMIN FRANKLIN

Haste makes waste.

He that goes a-borrowing
Soon goes a-sorrowing.

Waste not, want not.

SESQUI·CENTENNIAL·CELEBRATION
OF·THE·SIGNING·OF·THE
DECLARATION·OF·INDEPENDENCE

Ben and Me

from the book by

ROBERT LAWSON

After my dear friend Ben Franklin died, many so-called historians tried to write about his life, but they did not have the facts straight. Many of their stories are all wrong, so I feel the time has come for me to take pen in paw and set things right.

These so-called historians wrote pages and pages about Ben's great mind, his clear thinking, his fresh way of looking at things.

Had they asked me, I could have told them. It was **ME**.

For many years I was his closest friend and advisor, and, if I do say so myself, I played a large part in all that he did.

Not that I wish to take too much credit. I just hope to see credit given where credit is due, and that's to me—mostly.

Ben was truly a fine fellow, a great man, a good friend, and all that, but there is no getting around that he was not too bright at times, and had it not been for me—well, here's the true story. You can decide for yourself.

I, Amos, was the oldest of twenty-six children. With that number of mouths to feed, we were not a very well-to-do family of mice. In fact, we were really quite poor.

But it was not until the Hard Winter of 1745 that we found out just how cold and hungry a poor family of mice can get.

That was a winter long to be remembered. It was the coldest we had ever known. Night after night my poor father would come in tired and wet with his little sack almost empty.

Being the oldest, it seemed fitting that I should go out into the world. I hoped I could make my own way.

43

Maybe I could even find some way to help the others.

So, saying good-bye to my family, I set forth. It was the coldest night of that cold winter. Little did I dream that I would soon come to meet the great Dr. Franklin. All I thought of then were my cold paws and my empty stomach.

I have never known how far I went that night. What with being so cold and hungry, my thoughts were fuzzy. The first thing I remember clearly was being in a kitchen and smelling CHEESE! It didn't take long to find it, and it was only a tiny piece and fairly dry. But how I ate!

Then I began to look around the house. It was bare. Clean, but bare. A table and a few chairs, all hard and shiny. No soft things where a mouse could curl up and have a good warm nap. It was cold too, almost as cold as outdoors!

Upstairs were two rooms. One was dark, and from it came no sound. The other had a light, and the sound of sneezing. I chose the sneezy one.

In a large chair close to the fireplace sat a short, heavy, round-faced man. He was trying to write by the light of a candle. Every few minutes, he would sneeze, and his glasses would fly off. Reaching for them, he would drop his pen. By the time he found it, he would sneeze again. He was not getting much done in the way of writing.

Of course, I knew who he was. Everyone in Philadelphia knew the great Doctor Benjamin Franklin, statesman and writer.

He didn't look great that night, though. He just

looked cold—and a bit silly. He had his coat on indoors, trying to keep warm, and on his head was a big fuzzy fur cap.

The cap interested me, for I was still shaking from the cold, and this room was just as cold as the rest of the house. That funny-looking fur cap had a hole in one side of it. The hole was just about my size.

Up the back of the chair I went, and under cover of the next sneeze, in I slid. What a cozy place that was! Room to move about a bit, and just enough air. Such soft fur, and so warm!

"Here," I said to myself, "is my home. No more cold streets. Here I stay."

At that time, of course, I did not know how true that would turn out to be. All I knew was that I was warm, well fed, and—oh, so sleepy!

And so to bed.

• • • •

I slept late the next morning. When I awoke, my fur-cap home was at the foot of the bed, and I was in it.

Dr. Franklin was again at the fireplace, and he was still trying to write, between rounds of sneezing and glasses-hunting. The fire, what there was of it, was smoking, and the room was just as cold as ever.

"Not wishing to be picky—" I said. "But, maybe a bit more wood on that smoky pile that you seem to think is a fire might—"

"WASTE NOT, WANT NOT," said Dr. Franklin, and he went on writing.

"Well, just suppose," I said, "just suppose you spend two or three weeks in bed with a bad cold. Would that be a waste or—"

"Yes, it would be," said he, putting on a log, "whatever your name might be."

"Amos," said I, "and then there'd be doctors' bills—"

"BILLS!" said he, with an angry shake of his head. Quickly, he put on two more logs. They caught fire, and the room became a little warmer, but not much.

"Dr. Franklin," I said, "that fireplace is all wrong."

"You might call me Ben—just plain Ben," said he. "What's wrong with the fireplace?"

47

"Well, for one thing, most of the heat goes up the chimney, and for another, you can't get *around* it. Now, near where I used to live, there was a man who sold hot chestnuts on the street. Sometimes, when he was rushing, he'd drop a hot chestnut. My father was always on the look-out, and almost before that chestnut touched the ground, he'd have it in his sack. Then, home he'd rush with it. There, he'd put it in the middle of the floor, and we'd all gather around it to keep warm.

"It would heat all of us, and the room as well. It was all because it was OUT IN THE OPEN. It wasn't stuck in a hole in the wall like that fireplace."

"Amos," he shouted, "there's an idea there! But we couldn't move the fire out into the middle of the room."

"We could if there were something to put it in," said I.

"But the smoke?"

"PIPE," said I, and curled up for another nap.

I didn't get it, though.

Ben rushed off downstairs. In a minute he was back with a pile of junk. He dropped it on the floor and was off for more. No one could have slept.

After a few trips he had a big pile of things there. There were bricks and pieces of wire, some old warming pans, an oven, a wire birdcage, saws, nails, sand, pipes, hammers, and many other tools.

He drew out a plan and started to work. With all the noise he made, there was no chance of a nap, so I helped all I could, picking up the nails he dropped— and his glasses.

Ben was a tiger for work, once he was interested. It was almost noon before he stopped for a bit of rest. We looked over what had been done, and it didn't look bad.

It was shaped much like a small fireplace set up on legs. It had two doors in the front. There was a smoke pipe running from the back to the fireplace.

Ben walked around, looking at it. He was proud as could be, but worried.

"The floor," he said. "It's the floor that troubles me, Amos. With those short legs and that thin bottom, the heat—"

"I've been down to the shipyards," said I, "and I once heard a ship rat telling how a captain built a cooking fire on board. He put some sand right on the deck, bricks on top of that, and—"

"Amos!" he shouted. "You've got it!" He rushed for the bricks and sand, and he set to work again.

Soon it looked pretty promising.

When he finished, Ben stepped back to look at his work—and tripped over the saw. "Clean things up a bit, Amos, while I run and get some logs."

"Don't try to run," I said. "By the way, do you come through the kitchen on your way up?"

"Why?" he asked.

"In some ways, Ben," I said, "you're fairly bright, but in others you're not very sharp. The joy of building may be food and drink to you, but as for me, a bit of cheese—"

He was gone before I finished, but when he came back with the logs, he did have cheese and bread with him.

We put in some logs and lit her up. She worked fine. Ben was so proud and excited that I had to be rather sharp with him before he would sit down to eat. Even

51

then, he was up every minute, looking at his work from each corner.

Before we'd finished eating, the room had warmed up like a summer afternoon.

"Amos," said he, "we've done it!"

"Thanks for that WE," I said. "*We* means two, you and me. Now let's get things straight, Ben. Fame is nothing to me—cheese is. Also, there is my family to think about, twenty-five hungry brothers and sisters. I can be a great help to you. I've proved that. Now what do you propose?"

He looked like he was thinking pretty hard then, and I could feel a proverb coming on. At last it did. "THE LABORER IS WORTHY OF HIS HIRE," he said.

"I don't labor," I said. "I *think,* and proverbs don't fill empty stomachs. That's not a bad one, itself. Be exact."

Well, we talked it over for some time, and Ben was very fair. Really he was more than fair. I think that his being warm, for once, helped that.

Ben wrote it up that he would pay for bread and cheese for my family every week, and I would have his fur cap as my home. On my part, I was to be his advisor. I was to give him my best thinking and stay with him at all times. He was fine about the whole thing. I must say he lived up to it, too. Not once in all the rest of his life did he forget about that bread and cheese.

We signed the papers and shook hands.

After that, I couldn't help thinking how well things had gone for me that day. Here I was, warm and happy in a cozy home. My family was taken care of, and the great Ben Franklin was my friend.

After we sat around for a while, Ben said, "Amos. What shall we call this wonderful new thing we built?"

I said, "My friend, the credit is all yours. WE hereby call it the FRANKLIN stove."

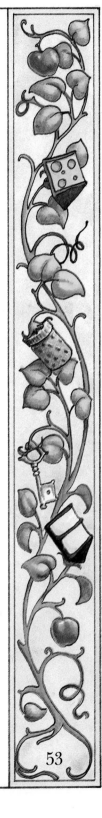

53

The Town Mouse and the Country Mouse

from

AESOP'S FABLES

A town mouse once upon a time went on a visit to his cousin in the country. He was rough and ready, this country cousin. But he was pleased to have the town mouse for a visit and made him very welcome. Good country fare of beans and bacon, cheese and bread, were all he had to offer, but he offered them freely.

The town mouse turned up his long nose at such plain foods. He said, "I cannot understand, Cousin, how you put up with such poor food as this. But of course, this is what you always eat in the country.

Now you come with me, and I will show you how to live. When you have been in town a week, you will wonder how you could ever have stood a country life."

No sooner said than done! The two mice set off for the town and reached the town mouse's house late at night. "You will want something to eat after our long trip," said the town mouse. He took his cousin into the grand dining room. There they found bits of food left over from a fine dinner. Soon the two mice were eating up jams and cakes and all that was nice.

Suddenly they heard growling and barking. Each moment it grew louder.

"What is that?" said the country mouse.

"It is only the dogs of the house," said the town mouse.

"Only!" said the country mouse. "I do not like that kind of noise with my dinner."

Just that minute the door flew open, in rushed two huge dogs, and the two mice had to leap down from the table and run for their lives.

"Good-bye, Cousin," said the country mouse.

"What! Going so soon?" said the other.

"Yes," he replied, thinking to himself:

"Better beans and bacon in peace
than cakes and jam in fear."

The Eagle

by

ALFRED, LORD TENNYSON

He clasps the crag with crooked hands,
Close to the sun in lonely lands,
Ringed with the azure world, he stands.

The wrinkled sea beneath him crawls.
He watches from his mountain walls—
And like a thunderbolt he falls.

I Watched an Eagle Soar

by

VIRGINIA DRIVING HAWK SNEVE

Grandmother,
I watched an eagle soar
high in the sky
until a cloud covered him up.
Grandmother,
I still saw the eagle
behind my eyes.

The Frogs Who Wanted a King

from

AESOP'S FABLES

The frogs had a happy life in the marsh, jumping and splashing about without a care in the world. But some of them were not satisfied. They thought they would be better off if they had a king to watch over them, so they asked Jupiter to send them a king.

Jupiter laughed at their request. He threw a huge log into their swamp and said, "Here is a king for you."

It landed with such a splash that it frightened many of the frogs, but soon they saw that it just lay still, so they approached the log. It did not move, so they jumped upon it.

Soon they were calling to Jupiter again. "Send us a real king. We want a king who is strong and powerful. Send us a king who will rule over us."

Jupiter grew tired of their croaking and said, "This time I will send you a different kind of king."

He sent them a strong and powerful stork, who at once started to gobble up the frogs.

In no time the frogs were crying to Jupiter again.

This time he sent his messenger Mercury to them, with a stern message. "You frogs asked me for a strong and powerful king. I gave you what you asked for, so now you will just have to make the best of it."

Leave well enough alone.

The Old Woman

by

BEATRIX POTTER

You know the old woman
Who lived in a shoe?
And had so many children
She didn't know what to do?

I think if she lived in
A little shoe-house—
That little old woman was
Surely a mouse!

Little Red Riding Hood and the Wolf

by

ROALD DAHL

As soon as Wolf began to feel
That he would like a decent meal,
He went and knocked on Grandma's door.
When Grandma opened it, she saw
The sharp white teeth, the horrid grin,
And Wolfie said, "May I come in?"

Poor Grandmamma was terrified.
"He's going to eat me up," she cried.
And she was absolutely right.
He ate her up in one big bite.

But Grandmamma was small and tough,
And Wolfie wailed, "That's not enough!
I haven't yet begun to feel
That I have had a decent meal!"
He ran around the kitchen yelping,
"I've got to have a second helping!"

Then added with a frightful leer,
"I'm therefore going to wait right here
Till Little Miss Red Riding Hood
Comes home from walking in the wood."

He quickly put on Grandma's clothes,
(Of course, he hadn't eaten those).
He dressed himself in coat and hat.
He put on shoes and after that
He even brushed and curled his hair,
Then sat himself in Grandma's chair.
In came the little girl in red.
She stopped. She stared. And then she said,

"What great big ears you have, Grandma."
"All the better to hear you with," the Wolf replied.
"What great big eyes you have, Grandma,"
    said Little Red Riding Hood.
"All the better to see you with," the Wolf replied.

65

He sat there watching her and smiled.
He thought, "I'm going to eat this child.
Compared with her old Grandmamma
She's going to taste like caviar."

Then Little Red Riding Hood said,
   "But, Grandmamma,
What a lovely great big furry coat you have on."

"That's wrong," cried Wolf. "Have you forgot
To tell me what BIG TEETH I've got?
Ah well, no matter what you say,
I'm going to eat you anyway."

The small girl smiles. One eyelid flickers.
She whips a pistol from her knickers.
She aims it at the creature's head
And bang, bang, bang, she shoots him dead.

A few weeks later in the wood,
I came across Miss Riding Hood.
But what a change! No cloak of red,
No silly hood upon her head.
She said, "Hello, and do please note
My lovely furry wolfskin coat."

Twinkle, Twinkle, Little Bat

from

ALICE'S ADVENTURES IN WONDERLAND

by

LEWIS CARROLL

Twinkle, twinkle, little bat,
How I wonder where you're at,
Up above the world so high
Like a tea tray in the sky.

67

UNIT TWO

Here and There,
Then and Now

Paul Revere's Ride

by

HENRY WADSWORTH LONGFELLOW

Listen, my children, and you shall hear
Of the midnight ride of Paul Revere,
On the eighteenth of April, in Seventy-five;
Hardly a man is now alive
Who remembers that famous day and year.

He said to his friend, "If the British march
By land or sea from the town to-night,
Hang a lantern aloft in the belfry-arch
Of the North Church tower as a signal light,—
One, if by land, and two, if by sea;
And I on the opposite shore will be
Ready to ride and spread the alarm
Through every Middlesex village and farm,
For the country-folk to be up and to arm."

Then he said "Good night!" and with muffled oar
Silently rowed to the Charlestown shore,
Just as the moon rose over the bay,
Where swinging wide at her moorings lay
The Somerset, British man-of-war;
A phantom ship, with each mast and spar
Across the moon like a prison-bar,
And a huge black hulk, that was magnified
By its own reflection in the tide.

Meanwhile, his friend, through alley and street,
Wanders and watches with eager ears,
Till in the silence around him he hears
The muster of men at the barrack-door,
The sound of arms, and the tramp of feet,
And the measured tread of the grenadiers,
Marching down to their boats on the shore.

Then he climbed to the tower of the Old North Church,
By the wooden stairs, with stealthy tread,
To the belfry-chamber overhead,
And started the pigeons from their perch
On the sombre rafters, that round him made
Masses and moving shapes of shade,—
By the trembling ladder, steep and tall,
To the highest window in the wall,
Where he paused to listen and look down
A moment on the roofs of the town,
And the moonlight flowing over all.

Beneath, in a churchyard, lay the dead,
In their night-encampment on the hill,
Wrapped in silence so deep and still
That he could hear like a sentinel's tread,
The watchful night-wind, as it went
Creeping along from tent to tent,
And seeming to whisper, "All is well!"
A moment only he feels the spell

Of the place and the hour, and the secret dread
Of the lonely belfry and the dead;
For suddenly all his thoughts are bent
On a shadowy something far away,
Where the river widens to meet the bay,—
A line of black that bends and floats
On the rising tide, like a bridge of boats.

Meanwhile, impatient to mount and ride
Booted and spurred, with a heavy stride
On the opposite shore walked Paul Revere.
Now he patted his horse's side,
Now gazed at the landscape far and near,
Then, impetuous, stamped the earth,
And turned and tightened his saddle-girth;
But mostly he watched with eager search

The belfry-tower of the Old North Church,
As it rose above the graves on the hill,
Lonely and spectral and sombre and still.
And lo! as he looks, on the belfry's height
He springs to the saddle, the bridle he turns,
But lingers, and gazes, till full on his sight
A second lamp in the belfry burns!

A hurry of hoofs in a village street,
A shape in the moonlight, a bulk in the dark,
And beneath, from the pebbles, in passing, a spark
Struck out by a steed flying fearless and fleet;
That was all! And yet, through the gloom
   and the light
The fate of a nation was riding that night;
And the spark struck out by that steed
   in his flight
Kindled the land into flames with its heat.

He has left the village and mounted the steep,
And beneath him, tranquil and broad and deep,
Is the Mystic, meeting the ocean tides;
And under the alders that skirt its edge,
Now soft on the sand now loud on the ledge,
Is heard the tramp of his steed as he rides.

It was twelve by the village clock
When he crossed the bridge into Medford town.
He heard the crowing of the cock,
And the barking of the farmer's dog,
And felt the damp of the river fog,
That rises after the sun goes down.

It was one by the village clock,
When he galloped into Lexington.
He saw the gilded weathercock
Swim in the moonlight as he passed,
And the meeting-house windows, blank and bare
Gaze at him with a spectral glare,
As if they already stood aghast
At the bloody work they would look upon.

It was two by the village clock,
When he came to the bridge in Concord town.
He heard the bleating of the flock,
And the twitter of birds among the trees,
And felt the breath of the morning breeze
Blowing over the meadows brown.
And one was safe and asleep in his bed
Who at the bridge would be first to fall,
Who that day would be lying dead,
Pierced by a British musket-ball.

You know the rest. In the books you have read
How the British Regulars fired and fled,—
How the farmers gave them ball for ball,
From behind each fence and farmyard wall,
Chasing the Redcoats down the lane,
Then crossing the fields to emerge again
Under the trees at the turn of the road
And only pausing to fire and load.

So through the night rode Paul Revere;
And so through the night went his cry of alarm
To every Middlesex village and farm,—
A cry of defiance and not of fear,
A voice in the darkness, a knock at the door,
And a word that shall echo forevermore!
For, borne on the night-wind of the Past,
Through all our history, to the last,
In the hour of darkness and peril and need,
The people will waken and listen to hear
The hurrying hoof-beats of that steed,
And the midnight message of Paul Revere.

One or Two?

by

BURR SHAFER

"Let me see—did Mr. Revere say, 'One if by land and two if by sea' or 'Two if by land and one if by sea?' "

The Bundle of Sticks

from

AESOP'S FABLES

A man had five sons who troubled him greatly because they were always fighting with each other. He kept telling them how much more they could get done if they stopped fighting and worked together, but they did not listen to him.

One day he called them to him and showed them a bundle of sticks. "Can you break this bundle?" he asked them.

Each son tried in turn. The oldest grabbed the ends of the sticks and pressed the bundle against his legs, but it was too heavy to bend.

The second son banged the bundle against the edge of a table, but the sticks did not crack.

The third and fourth sons jumped on the bundle, but it did not break.

The youngest son put his knee on the bundle and pulled the ends with his arms, but the sticks did not even bend.

83

Then the father untied the bundle and lined up the sticks on the table. "Now break the sticks," he said, "one by one."

His sons had no trouble.

"My boys," he said. "Each of you alone is weak, like one stick. But together you are strong, like the bundle of sticks."

United we stand; divided we fall.

85

Color

by

LANGSTON HUGHES

Wear it
Like a banner
For the proud—
Not like a shroud
Wear it
Like a song
Soaring high—
Not moan or cry.

I Have a Dream

from a speech by

MARTIN LUTHER KING, JR.

I say to you today, my friends, even though we face the difficulties of today and tomorrow, I still have a dream. It is a dream deeply rooted in the American Dream. I have a dream that one day this nation will rise up and live out the true meaning of its creed: "We hold these truths to be self-evident, that all men are created equal."

I have a dream that one day on the red hills of Georgia the sons of former slaves and the sons of former slave-owners will be able to sit down together at the table of brotherhood.

I have a dream that one day even the state of Mississippi, a state sweltering with the heat of injustice and oppression, will be transformed into an oasis of freedom and justice.

I have a dream that my four little children will one day live in a nation where they will not be judged by the color of their skin but by the content of their character.

I have a dream today.

I have a dream that one day down in Alabama . . . little black boys and little black girls will be able to join hands with little white boys and white girls as sisters and brothers.

I have a dream today.

I have a dream that one day every valley shall be exalted, every hill and mountain shall be made low. The rough places will be made plain and the crooked places will be made straight. . . .

This is my hope and this is the faith with which I go back to the South. With this faith we will be able to hew out of the mountain of despair a stone of hope. . . . With this faith we will be able to work together, to pray together, to struggle together . . . to stand up for freedom together knowing that we will be free one day.

This will be the day when all of God's children will be able to sing with new meaning . . . "let freedom ring." Let freedom ring from the hilltops of New Hampshire. Let freedom ring from the mighty mountains of New York. Let freedom ring from the snow-capped Rockies of Colorado. But not only that, let freedom ring from Stone Mountain of Georgia and Lookout Mountain of Tennessee—from every hill and molehill and from every mountainside.

When we allow freedom to ring—when we let it ring from every village and every hamlet, from every state and every city, we will be able to speed up that day when all of God's children, black men and white men, Jews and gentiles, Protestants and Catholics, will be able to join hands and sing in the words of the Negro spiritual, "Free at last, Free at last, Thank God Almighty, we are free at last."

Two Big Bears

from

LITTLE HOUSE IN THE BIG WOODS

by

LAURA INGALLS WILDER

In the Big Woods the snow was beginning to melt. Bits of it dropped from the branches of the trees and made little holes in the softer snow below. At noon all the big icicles hanging from the roof of the little house had drops of water at their tips.

Pa said he must go to town to sell the furs of the wild animals he had been trapping all winter, so one evening he made a big bundle of them. There were so many furs that when they were packed tightly and tied together they made a bundle almost as big as Pa.

Very early one morning Pa tied the bundle of furs on his shoulders, and started to walk to town. There were so many furs to carry that he could not take his gun.

Ma was worried, but Pa said that by starting before sunup and walking very fast all day he could get home again before dark.

The nearest town was far away. Laura and Mary had never seen a town. They had never seen a store. They had never seen even two houses standing together, but they knew that in a town there were many houses, and a store full of candy and cloth and other wonderful things.

They knew that Pa would sell his furs to the storekeeper for beautiful things from town, and all day they were waiting for the presents he would bring them.

When the sun sank low above the treetops and no more drops fell from the tips of the icicles, they began to watch for Pa.

The sun sank out of sight. The woods grew dark, and he did not come. Ma started supper and set the table. But he did not come. It was time to do the dishes, and still he had not come.

Ma said that Laura might come with her while she milked the cow. Laura could carry the lantern.

93

So Laura put on her coat. She was proud to be helping Ma with the milking, and she carried the lantern very carefully. It had places cut in its sides for the light to shine through.

When Laura walked behind Ma on the path to the barn, the little bits of light from the lantern leaped all around her on the snow. The night was not yet quite dark. The woods were dark, but there was a gray light on the snowy path and in the sky there were a few stars. The stars did not look as warm and bright as the little lights that came from the lantern.

Laura was surprised to see the dark shape of Sukey, the brown cow, standing at the barnyard gate. Ma was surprised, too.

It was too early in the spring for Sukey to be let out in the Big Woods to eat grass. She lived in the barn, but sometimes on warmer days Pa let her come into the barnyard. Now Ma and Laura saw her behind the bars, waiting for them.

Ma went up to the gate and pushed against it to open it, but it did not open very far, because there was Sukey, standing against it.

Ma said, "Sukey, get over!" She reached across the gate and slapped Sukey's shoulder.

Just then one of the dancing little bits of light from the lantern jumped between the bars of the

gate, and Laura saw long, black fur and two hard, little glassy eyes.

Sukey had thin, short, brown fur. Sukey had large, soft eyes.

Ma said, "Laura, walk back to the house."

So Laura turned around and began to walk toward the house. Ma came behind her. When they had gone part way, Ma picked her up, lantern and all, and ran. Ma ran with her into the house, and slammed the door.

Then Laura said, "Ma, was it a bear?"

"Yes, Laura," Ma said. "It was a bear."

Laura began to cry as she hung on to Ma. "Oh, will he eat Sukey?"

"No," said Ma, hugging her. "Sukey is safe in the barn. Think, Laura, all those big heavy logs in the barn walls and the door is heavy, too, made to keep bears out. No, the bear cannot get in and eat Sukey."

Laura felt better then. "But he could have hurt us, couldn't he?" she asked.

"He didn't hurt us," Ma said. "You were a good girl, Laura, to do exactly as I told you, and to do it quickly, without asking why."

Ma was shaking, and she began to laugh a little. "To think," she said, "I've slapped a bear."

Then she put supper on the table for Laura and Mary. Pa had not come yet. He didn't come. Ma said Laura and Mary had to go to bed, so they did.

Ma sat by the window, patching Pa's shirt. The house seemed cold and still and strange, without Pa.

Laura listened to the wind in the Big Woods. All around the house the wind went crying as though it were lost in the dark and the cold. The wind sounded frightened.

Ma finished the patch on Pa's shirt. Laura saw her fold it slowly and carefully. She smoothed it with her hand.

Then Ma did a thing she had never done before. She went to the door and pulled the leather latch string through its hole in the door. That way, nobody could get in from outside until she lifted the latch.

She saw that Laura and Mary were still awake and she said to them, "Go to sleep, girls. Everything is all right. Pa will be here in the morning."

Then she went back to her rocking chair. She was sitting up late, waiting for Pa, and Laura and Mary meant to stay awake, too, until he came. But at last they went to sleep.

In the morning Pa was there. He had brought candy for Laura and Mary, and two pieces of pretty cloth so that Ma could make them each a dress. Mary's was blue and white. Laura's was dark red with little golden dots on it. Ma had cloth for a dress too. It was light brown. They were all happy that Pa had brought them such beautiful presents.

The tracks of the big bear were all around the barn, but Sukey and the horses were safe inside.

All that day the sun was shining. The snow melted, and little streams of water ran from the icicles, which all the time grew thinner. Before the sun set that night, the bear tracks could no longer be seen in the wet, soft snow.

97

After supper Pa told Laura and Mary that he had a new story for them. "It's 'The Story of Pa and the Bear in the Way,'" he said.

"When I went to town yesterday with the furs, I found it hard walking in the soft snow. It took me a long time to get to town. The other men with furs had come in earlier, so the store keeper was busy, and I had to wait. Then it took time to pick out the things I wanted to bring back to you, so it was nearly sundown before I could start home.

"The walking was hard and I was tired, so I had not gone far before night came. There I was, alone in the Big Woods without my gun. There were still six miles to walk, and I came along as fast as I could.

"The night grew darker and darker, and I wished for my gun, because I knew that some of the bears had just come out of their dens. I had seen their tracks that morning.

"Bears are hungry and cross at this time of year. They've been sleeping all winter long with nothing to eat, and that makes them thin and angry when they wake up. I did not want to meet one.

"I hurried along as quick as I could in the dark. By and by the stars gave a little light. In some spots it was too dark to see anything, but in the open places I could see the snowy road ahead a little way.

"All this time I was watching for bears.

"Then I came again into an open place. At the other end of the clearing, right in the middle of the road, I saw a big, black bear.

"He was standing up on his back legs, looking at me.

"My hair stood straight up. I stopped in my tracks, and stood still. The bear did not move. There he stood, blocking the way.

"I knew it would do no good to try to go around him. He would follow me into the dark woods where he could see better than I could.

"How I wished for my gun! I had to pass that bear, to get home. I thought that if I could scare him, he might get out of the road and let me go by. So I took a deep breath, and suddenly I shouted with all my might, and stepped toward him, waving my arms.

"He didn't move.

"I did not want to get too close, I'll tell you. I wanted more space between that bear and me, so I stepped back very slowly. I stopped and looked at him, and he stood, looking at me.

"Well, it would do me no good to run away since there were other bears in the woods. I might meet one any time, so I might as well face up to this one. Besides, I was coming home to Ma and you girls.

99

I would never get here if I ran away from everything that scared me. So at last I looked around, and I got a big club. It was a branch that had broken off a tree because the snow was so heavy on it.

"I lifted it up in my hands, and I ran straight at that bear. I swung my club as hard as I could and brought it down, bang! on his head.

"And there he still stood, for he was nothing but a big, black, burned stump!

"I had passed it on my way to town that morning. It wasn't a bear at all. I only thought it was a bear, because I'd been thinking all the time about bears and being afraid I'd meet one."

"It really wasn't a bear at all?" Mary asked.

"No, Mary, it wasn't a bear at all. There I had been yelling, and dancing, and waving my arms, all by myself in the Big Woods, trying to scare a stump!"

Laura said, "Ours was really a bear, but we were not scared, because we thought it was Sukey."

Pa did not say anything, but he hugged her tighter.

"Oo-oo! That bear might have eaten Ma and me all up!" said Laura. "But Ma walked right up to him and slapped him, and he didn't do anything at all. Why didn't he do anything?"

"I guess he was too surprised to do anything, Laura," Pa said. "I guess he was too afraid when the lantern shined in his eyes. Then, when Ma walked up to him and slapped him, he knew *she* wasn't afraid."

"Well, you were brave, too," Laura said. "Even if it was only a stump, you thought it was a bear. You'd have hit him on the head with a club, if he had been a bear, wouldn't you, Pa?"

"Yes," said Pa. "I would. You see, I had to. It was the only way I could get home to Ma and you girls."

• • • • •

You can read more about Laura and her family in *Little House in the Big Woods* and in the other *Little House* books.

101

Why the Bear Is Stumpy-Tailed

a Norwegian folktale retold by

GEORGE WEBBE DASENT

One day the bear met the fox, who was carrying a string of fish he had stolen.

"Where did you get those fish?" asked the bear.

"Oh, I've been out fishing and I caught them," said the fox.

So the bear had a mind to learn to fish too. He asked the fox to tell him how he was to set about it.

"It will be easy for you," said the fox. "You've only got to go out upon the ice that covers the lake. Cut a hole in the ice and stick your tail down into it. You must go on holding it there as long as you can. You are not to mind if your tail smarts a little. That's when the fish bite."

"I see," said the bear. "And how long must I stay?"

"The longer you hold your tail down in the water, the more fish you'll get. Then, all at once, out with it. Give your tail a quick cross-pull, sideways. And make it a strong pull, too."

The bear did as the fox had said. He held his tail a long, long time down in the hole, until it was frozen. Then he tried to pull it out with a quick cross-pull. And it snapped right off.

That's why the bear goes about with a stumpy tail, even to this very day.

He Lion, Bruh Bear, and Bruh Rabbit

by

VIRGINIA HAMILTON

ay that he Lion would get up each and every mornin. Stretch and walk around. He'd roar, "ME AND MYSELF. ME AND MYSELF," like that. Scare all the little animals so they were afraid to come outside in the sunshine. Afraid to go huntin or fishin or whatever the little animals wanted to do.

"What we gone do about it?" they asked one another. Squirrel leapin from branch to branch, just scared. Possum playin dead, couldn't hardly move him.

He Lion just went on, stickin out his chest and roarin, "ME AND MYSELF. ME AND MYSELF."

The little animals held a sit-down talk, and one by one and two by two and all by all, they decide to go see Bruh Bear and Bruh Rabbit. For they know that Bruh Bear been around. And Bruh Rabbit say he has, too.

So they went to Bruh Bear and Bruh Rabbit. Said, "We have some trouble. Old he Lion, him scarin everybody, roarin every mornin and all day, 'ME AND MYSELF. ME AND MYSELF,' like that."

"Why he Lion want to do that?" Bruh Bear said.

"Is that all he Lion have to say?" Bruh Rabbit asked.

"We don't know why, but that's all he Lion can tell us and we didn't ask him to tell us that," said the little animals. "And him scarin the children with it. And we wish him to stop it."

"Well, I'll go see him, talk to him. I've known he Lion a long kind of time," Bruh Bear said.

"I'll go with you," said Bruh Rabbit. "I've known he Lion most long as you."

That bear and that rabbit went off through the forest. They kept hearin somethin. Mumble, mumble. Couldn't make it out. They got farther in the forest. They heard it plain now. "ME AND MYSELF. ME AND MYSELF."

"Well, well, well," said Bruh Bear. He wasn't scared. He'd been around the whole forest, seen a lot.

"My, my, my," said Bruh Rabbit. He'd seen enough to know not to be afraid of an old he lion. Now old he lions could be dangerous, but you had to know how to handle them.

The bear and the rabbit climbed up and up the cliff where he Lion had his lair. They found him. Kept their distance. He watchin them and they watchin him. Everybody actin cordial.

"Hear tell you are scarin everybody, all the little animals, with your roarin all the time," Bruh Rabbit said.

"I roars when I pleases," he Lion said.

"Well, might could you leave off the noise first thing in the mornin, so the little animals can get what they want to eat and drink?" asked Bruh Bear.

"Listen," said he Lion, and then he roared: "ME AND MYSELF. ME AND MYSELF. Nobody tell me what not to do," he said. "I'm the king of the forest, *me and myself.*"

"Better had let me tell you somethin," Bruh Rabbit said, "for I've seen Man, and I know him the real king of the forest."

He Lion was quiet awhile. He looked straight through that scrawny lil Rabbit like he was nothin atall. He looked at Bruh Bear and figured he'd talk to him.

"You, Bear, you been around," he Lion said.

"That's true," said old Bruh Bear. "I been about everywhere. I've been around the whole forest."

"Then you must know somethin," he Lion said.

"I know lots," said Bruh Bear, slow and quiet-like.

"Tell me what you know about Man," he Lion said. "He think him the king of the forest?"

"Well, now, I'll tell you," said Bruh Bear, "I been around, but I haven't ever come across Man that I know of. Couldn't tell you nothin about him."

So he Lion had to turn back to Bruh Rabbit. He didn't want to but he had to. "So what?" he said to that lil scrawny hare.

"Well, you got to come down from there if you want to see Man," Bruh Rabbit said. "Come down from there and I'll show you him."

He Lion thought a minute, an hour, and a whole day. Then, the next day, he came on down.

He roared just once, "ME AND MYSELF. ME AND MYSELF. Now," he said, "come show me Man."

So they set out. He Lion, Bruh Bear, and Bruh Rabbit. They go along and they go along, rangin the forest. Pretty soon, they come to a clearin. And playin in it is a little fellow about nine years old.

"Is that there Man?" asked he Lion.

"Why no, that one is called Will Be, but it sure is not Man," said Bruh Rabbit.

So they went along and they went along. Pretty soon, they come upon a shade tree. And sleepin under it is an old, olden fellow, about ninety years olden.

"There must lie Man," spoke he Lion. "I knew him wasn't gone be much."

"That's not Man," said Bruh Rabbit. "That fellow is Was Once. You'll know it when you see Man."

So they went on along. He Lion is gettin tired of strollin. So he roars, "ME AND MYSELF. ME AND MYSELF."

Upsets Bear so that Bear doubles over and runs and climbs a tree.

"Come down from there," Bruh Rabbit tellin him. So after a while Bear comes down. He keepin his distance from he Lion, anyhow. And they set out some more. Goin along quiet and slow.

In a little while they come to a road. And comin on way down the road, Bruh Rabbit sees Man comin. Man about twenty-one years old. Big and strong, with a big gun over his shoulder.

"There!" Bruh Rabbit says. "See there, he Lion? There's Man. You better go meet him."

"I will," says he Lion. And he sticks out his chest and he roars, "ME AND MYSELF. ME AND MYSELF." All the way to Man he's roarin proud, "ME AND MYSELF. ME AND MYSELF!"

"Come on, Bruh Bear, let's go!" Bruh Rabbit says.

"What for?" Bruh Bear wants to know.

"You better come on!" And Bruh Rabbit takes ahold of Bruh Bear and half drags him to a thicket. And there he makin the Bear hide with him.

For here comes Man. He sees old he Lion real good now. He drops to one knee and he takes aim with his big gun.

Old he Lion is roarin his head off: "ME AND MYSELF! ME AND MYSELF!"

The big gun goes off: PA-LOOOM!

He Lion falls back hard on his tail.

The gun goes off again. PA-LOOOM!

He Lion is flyin through the air. He lands in the thicket.

"Well, did you see Man?" asked Bruh Bear.

"I seen him," said he Lion. "Man spoken to me unkind, and got a great long stick him keepin on his shoulder. Then Man taken that stick down and him speakin real mean. Thunderin at me and lightnin comin from that stick, awful bad. Made me sick. I had to turn around. And Man pointin that stick again and thunderin at me some more. So I come in here, cause it seem like him throwed some stickers at me each time it thunder, too."

"So you've met Man, and you know zactly what that kind of him is," says Bruh Rabbit.

"I surely do know that," he Lion said back.

Awhile after he Lion met Man, things were some better in the forest. Bruh Bear knew what Man looked like so he could keep out of his way. That rabbit always did know to keep out of Man's way. The little animals could go out in the mornin because he Lion was more peaceable. He didn't walk around roarin at the top of his voice all the time. And when he Lion did lift that voice of his, it was like, "Me and Myself and Man. Me and Myself and Man." Like that.

Wasn't too loud atall.

• • • •

Animal tales are the most widely known black folk-tales. Because of the menial labor slaves were made to do,

they observed and came to know many kinds of animals throughout their daily lives. They developed a keen interest in these lowly creatures. Because they had so little knowledge about the fauna they found here, they made up tales that to some extent explained and fit their observations of animal behavior. Furthermore, the tales satisfied the slaves' need to explain symbolically and secretly the ruling behavior of the slaveowners in relation to themselves. As time passed, the tales were told more for entertainment and instruction.

"He Lion, Bruh Bear, and Bruh Rabbit" is a typical tale of an animal, whether it is wolf, lion, bear, rabbit, goat, tiger, etc., that learns through experience to fear man. It is the rabbit that shows man to the lion. And the rabbit, representing the slave in the animal tales, knows from experience to fear man. The tale ranges throughout North and South America, Europe, and Africa.

Tommy

by

GWENDOLYN BROOKS

I put a seed into the ground
And said, "I'll watch it grow."
I watered it and cared for it
As well as I could know.

One day I walked in my back yard,
And oh, what did I see!
My seed had popped itself right out,
Without consulting me.

113

Johnny Appleseed, 1775–1847

by

ROSEMARY CARR BENÉT

Of Jonathan Chapman
Two things are known,
That he loved apples,
That he walked alone.

At seventy-odd
He was gnarled as could be,
But ruddy and sound
As a good apple tree.

For fifty years over
Of harvest and dew,
He planted his apples
Where no apples grew.

The winds of the prairie
Might blow through his rags,
But he carried his seeds
In the best deerskin bags.

From old Ashtabula
To frontier Fort Wayne,
He planted and pruned
And he planted again.

He had not a hat
To encumber his head.
He wore a tin pan
On his white hair instead.

He nested with owl,
And with bear-cub and possum,
And knew all his orchards
Root, tendril and blossom.

A fine old man,
As ripe as a pippin,
His heart still light,
And his step still skipping.

The stalking Indian,
The beast in its lair
Did no hurt
While he was there.

For they could tell,
As wild things can,
That Jonathan Chapman
Was God's own man.

Why did he do it?
We do not know.
He wished that apples
Might root and grow.

He has no statue.
He has no tomb.
He has his apple trees
Still in bloom.

Consider, consider,
Think well upon
The marvelous story
Of Appleseed John.

The Banyan Deer

from

THE JATAKA TALES

by

ELLEN C. BABBITT

There was once a Deer the color of gold. His eyes were like round jewels, and his horns were as white as silver. His mouth was red like a flower, and his hoofs were bright and hard. He had a large body and a fine tail. He lived in a forest and was king of a herd of five hundred Banyan Deer.

Nearby lived another herd of deer called Monkey Deer, and they, too, had a king.

The Rajah of that country was fond of hunting the Deer and eating deer meat. He did not like to go alone so he called the people of his town to go with him, day after day.

The townspeople did not like this, for while they were gone no one did their work, so they decided to make a park and drive the Deer into it. Then their Rajah could go into the park and hunt, and they could go on with their daily work.

They made a park and planted grass in it. Then they built a fence all around it, drove the Deer into it, and showed it to their Rajah.

He went in at once to look at the Deer. First he met with the two Deer kings, and he granted them their lives. Then he looked at their great herds and knew what fine meals he would be having.

Some days he would go to hunt the Deer, and sometimes his cook would go. As soon as any of the Deer saw them, they would shake with fear and run. Some would get away, but some would be wounded. And some were hit and would drop down dead.

The King of the Banyan Deer sent for the King of the Monkey Deer and said, "Friend, many of our Deer are being killed. And many others are being wounded. After this, suppose one from my herd goes up to be killed one day, and the next day let one from your herd go up. Fewer Deer will be lost this way."

The King of the Monkey Deer agreed.

119

So, each day the Deer whose turn it was would go and lie down, placing its head on the block. The cook would come and carry off the one he found lying there.

One day the lot fell to a mother in the Monkey Deer herd who had a young baby. She went to her king and said, "Oh, King of the Monkey Deer, let the turn pass me by until my baby is old enough to get along without me. Then I will go and put my head on the block."

But the king did not help her. He told her that if the lot had fallen to her, she must die.

Then she went to the King of the Banyan Deer and asked him to save her.

"Go back to your herd. I will go in your place," he said.

The next day the cook found the King of the Banyan Deer lying with his head on the block. The cook went to the Rajah, who came himself to find out about this.

"King of the Banyan Deer!" exclaimed the Rajah. "Did I not grant you your life? Why are you lying here?"

"Oh, great Rajah," said the King of the Banyan Deer. "A mother came to me with her young baby and told me that the lot had fallen to her. I could not ask anyone else to take her place, so I came myself."

"King of the Banyan Deer! I never saw such kindness and mercy. Rise up. I will grant your life and hers, and I will no longer hunt any of the Deer in either park or forest."

• • • •

The Jataka Tales are fables and folktales from India. They have been retold since the second century B.C.

The Stone Cutter of the Orient

by

CAROLYN SHERWIN BAILEY

Long ago in the Orient there was a stone cutter who hurried across the rice fields every morning to his work on the mountainside. He would take his sharp tools with him and tap, tap, tap at the stone of the mountain.

When he had chipped off a large piece of rock, he would work on it far into the night. It had to be smooth and beautiful, and just the right shape for builders to use. He was proud of his work and happy with it.

But one day, when he carried a finely cut block of stone to the house of the richest man in the city, he saw all kinds of beautiful things—such as he had never dreamed of.

"Oh," he cried. "I wish I were this rich. I wish I might sleep in a bed soft as down and eat from dishes of silver and gold."

Then he picked up his tools and started home. But the mountain spirit had heard his wish.

123

Instead of the home he had left in the morning,
there stood a wonderful new house. It was as full
of beautiful things as the house of the richest man
in the city. The stone cutter slept that night on a bed
as soft as down, and the next day he ate from dishes
of silver and gold.

As he sat in his new house, he decided not to work
any more. He would just sit by the window and watch
others work.

While he was watching, he saw a prince come
along in a fine carriage pulled by snow-white horses.
There were servants running on each side, holding
a golden canopy over the head of the prince.

"Oh!" said the stone cutter. "I wish I were a
prince. I want to ride in a carriage with a golden
canopy carried over my head."

And no sooner had he wished it than it came to
pass—he was a prince. Now his home was a castle. He
had servants dressed in red and gold. He had a huge
garden with a fountain in the middle of it, and he
drove through the streets with a canopy held over him
to keep off the sun. So for a little while he was happy.

But one day he went out to his garden with the
fountain in the middle of it, and he saw that the sun
was drying up his grass, in spite of all the water
he had ordered to be put on it.

"The sun is mightier than I!" he cried. "I would be the sun."

Again the mountain spirit heard him—the stone cutter was changed into the sun. He felt very proud and mighty, so large and yellow and high. He burned the rice fields, and he shone down on the rich people and the poor people alike.

He was happy until the day that a cloud covered his face, and he could not shine down on anyone.

"The cloud is mightier than I!" he cried. "I would be the cloud."

So the mountain spirit changed him into a cloud, and he lay for a while between the sun and the earth. He sent rain to the earth and made the grass green, but that was not enough for him.

He began pouring down rain for days, until the rivers ran over their banks and the rice fields were under water. He washed away whole towns and villages. But there was one thing he could not move—the great rock on the mountainside.

"Is the mountain stronger than I?" he cried. "I will be the mountain!"

At once the mountain spirit changed him into rock. For years he stood, proudly raising his head to the sky. Nothing could move him—not the burning of the sun, not the downpouring of the rain.

127

"This is better than anything else!" he cried.
"I am the mountain, and I am the mightiest of all!"

But one day he heard a sharp tap, tap, tapping at his feet, and he saw a stone cutter there, working with his sharp tools and driving them into the mountainside. As the stone cutter chipped away at him, he felt a strange fear deep inside.

"The stone cutter is mightier than I!" cried the mountain. "I would be that man."

So he became a man once more—the same stone cutter he was at the beginning, but a wiser man. He still worked from morning until night. Yet he stayed happy now, for he knew that when he was at his work, he was the mightiest of all.

Men and Mountains

by

WILLIAM BLAKE

Great things are done
    when men and mountains meet.
This is not done by jostling in the street.

Hide and Seek

by

ROBERT GRAVES

The trees are tall, but the moon small,
My legs feel rather weak,
For Avis, Mavis and Tom Clarke
Are hiding somewhere in the dark
And it's my turn to seek.

Suppose they lay a trap and play
A trick to frighten me?
Suppose they plan to disappear
And leave me here, half-dead with fear,
Groping from tree to tree.

Alone, alone, all on my own
And then perhaps to find
Not Avis, Mavis and young Tom
But monsters to run shrieking from,
Mad monsters of no kind?

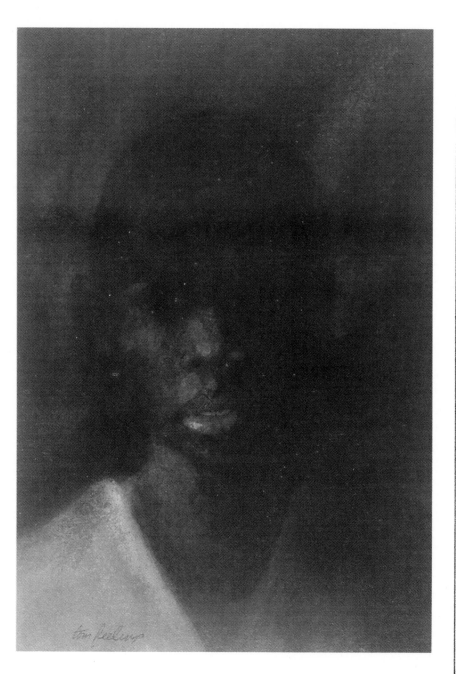

131

The Bat

by

THEODORE ROETHKE

By day the bat is cousin to the mouse.
He likes the attic of an aging house.

His fingers make a hat about his head.
His pulse-beat is so slow we think him dead.

He loops in crazy figures half the night
Among the trees that face the corner light.

But when he brushes up against a screen,
We are afraid of what our eyes have seen.

For something is amiss or out of place
When mice with wings can wear a human face.

133

America's Own Mark Twain

by

JEANETTE EATON

Mark Twain, whose real name was Sam Clemens, is well known and well loved as the author of *The Adventures of Tom Sawyer.* That book was based on his own boyhood in Hannibal, Missouri. Sam Clemens and his friend Tom Blankenship actually had some of the adventures that later appeared in books written under Sam's pen name "Mark Twain." This part of Sam Clemens's biography shows how much he had in common with the character Tom Sawyer.

George F. Fuller
A Steamboat Race on the Mississippi (Between the Baltic and the Diana)
Missouri Historical Society

The Mississippi River gave Sam Clemens a place for adventures, often mixed with strange and even frightening times. In the fall of 1843, for example, Sam's day on the river ended in a night of terror.

On his way home from school that day, Sam met Tom Blankenship. Tom was the most envied boy in Hannibal, Missouri. He didn't go to school. He went barefoot from early spring until snowfall. He could fish, swim, and paddle a canoe all day if he chose.

On the other hand, Tom had no mother, and his father often beat him in a drunken rage. He went about unwashed. He dressed in rags, and sometimes he went hungry.

Besides, all the mothers of well-brought-up children in Hannibal were against having their children spend any time with Tom Blankenship. So it was special fun to seek his company. Tom was easygoing and pleasant. But he had learned more than most boys his age about how to take care of himself. Sam Clemens was happy to see him.

"Hi, Tom. Where you going?" asked Sam.

"Oh, fishing, I reckon," said Tom. "I found a skiff that was washed up on shore in the storm last week. Wish you didn't have to go home and could come along."

"Shucks, I'll come," said Sam. "I'll just get home late."

It was a perfect afternoon. Sam Clemens liked to be on the Mississippi River better than anywhere else in the world. Each boy caught two fish. In the later afternoon they landed, built a fire, and cooked the fish. After a swim, they stretched out on the grass. Sunset clouds drifted over them as they talked, and later a moon rose over the trees.

"Say, Tom," Sam Clemens said suddenly. "Do you suppose your pa knows where you are?"

"Nope," Tom Blankenship answered. "Anyway, he wouldn't care where I was, except maybe he wants me to fetch him a bottle. What about your folks?"

Sam confessed that probably Mr. and Mrs. Clemens and all the rest of his family were combing the town to find him. In his mind he pictured his arrival at home and the storm of fussing that would meet him. It was just too much to face.

"I know what I'll do," said Sam. "I won't go home at all. I'll crawl into my pa's law office and sleep there. Maybe in the morning they'll be so glad I ain't drowned that they'll let me off easy."

Tom Blankenship nodded. "That's a good idea," he said.

At the corner of two shadowy streets, they parted with whispered farewells.

Sam Clemens found it easy to push up a window in his father's small office. An old couch stood right beside it. Kicking off his shoes, Sam stretched out and was asleep in a few seconds.

Perhaps it was the bright moonlight streaming in at the window that woke him. He sat up with a jerk, looked around, and stared in surprise for a moment at the room. Then he remembered why he was in his father's law office instead of at home in his bed.

But what was that on the floor? Choking down a scream, the boy stared at the man's figure stretched out full length on the wooden boards. Who was it? Was he asleep? He couldn't be a robber.

Just as Sam was able to breathe again, moonlight flooded down on the still figure. Oh, heavens! It couldn't be! What he saw was the marble face of a dead man!

Sam got into his shoes and crawled out of the window. Up the moonlit streets he ran, racing to his house as fast as he could go. No light shone in the Clemens house.

The Clemens house in Hannibal, Missouri

137

He climbed up on the porch and found his bedroom window wide open.

Without making a sound, he eased himself inside. Then he stripped off his clothes and lay down, trying to keep his tense body from jerking and thrashing around as he lay there, sleepless.

Next morning, he screwed up his courage to face his parents. To his surprise, questions and comments were brief. Unasked, they told him of a shocking murder. Two travelers had hardly landed in Hannibal when they started a drunken fight. Knives were flashed and one was driven through the heart of the smaller man.

Sam Clemens's father came on the scene in time to have the killer caught and dragged into the jail. Mr. Clemens then said the dead man could be placed in his empty office until morning. Today the killer would be charged with the crime.

Sam listened with his stomach rising and falling. He knew he was going to be haunted by the dead man's ghost. And so he was, in uneasy dreams and nightmares, for quite some time.

Around that same time, Sam got his first look at one of the wonders of Hannibal, its famous cave. On a picnic he was allowed to join a group on a visit to the cave.

A walk straight up a hill brought them to the entrance on its steep side. A heavy door of oak had been opened for visitors, and they walked into the large entrance hall. Sam's wondering eyes turned from the uneven rocky floor to the dripping walls and up to the rough ceiling.

"Oh, it's a big cave, ain't it!" he exclaimed.

A girl in the group giggled. "Big! Why, it's miles long and miles deep. Nobody's ever been all through it. Just wait until we light our candles and you'll see."

Down the sloping passage went the group, with candles lifted high to shine on the wet walls. They moved slowly. Sam was shown how one narrow path after another led off the main path.

They turned right into a huge room hollowed out of solid rock. Then they had to retrace their steps. Laughter and talk echoed in the darkness. But as they kept going down, down, down, Sam felt they must have reached the very center of the earth.

"Couldn't you get lost in this cave?" Sam asked.

He was told that you could indeed. For this reason, groups of visitors always kept close together and carried plenty of candles. Some few persons had managed to find lakes and streams underground.

139

Others had come upon cliffs that dropped down to fearful depths. One wrong step on the wet slippery path might mean death.

Sam Clemens said nothing in reply. But that night he remarked to his mother that he meant to explore the cave from top to bottom some day.

At the time Mrs. Clemens only laughed at her son. But some time later she remembered his boast with a sinking heart.

One morning her friend Mrs. Bowen came in with frightening news. Her son Will had let it slip that several times after school he had been exploring the cave with Sam Clemens.

"Imagine those two young fools!" gasped Will Bowen's mother. "You just know that they'll get lost some day, sure as you live, if not drowned or smashed up in a fall in that cave. What are we going to do?"

Mrs. Clemens heard this report with fear and anger. For half an hour the two women talked about their worries, which was lucky for Sam. By the time he got home for lunch, his mother had talked out most of her anger. She greeted her son in a mood of loving concern.

"Oh, Sam," she concluded, with a sob in her voice. "Do you want to break my heart? Last year you nearly drowned trying to swim in the river during a storm. Now you want to get lost forever in the cave."

Entrance to the Mark Twain Cave

Surprised as he was that his visits to the cave were no longer a secret, Sam was touched by his mother's concern.

"Oh, Ma," he said. "Don't talk so. We won't get lost. We do just the way Theseus did in the myth when he went through the maze after that monster, the Minotaur. You remember—his lady gave him a string, and she kept one end herself at the door. All Theseus had to do after killing the Minotaur was to go back the way the string led. We tie a strong kite string to a piece of rock on the main path and unwind it while we explore. Then we follow it back again. We always keep close together. So don't you worry!"

Mrs. Clemens was not impressed. She told him never to enter the cave again, and she wanted him to give her his word that he would obey.

Sam knew better than to defy her outright. What he must do was wiggle out of answering somehow. And by luck, he had the perfect means of doing it right in his pocket.

With a big smile he said, "I'm sorry you got so scared about me, Ma. I think a lot of you, Ma. I've got a present for you in my pocket. Hold out your hand."

Smiling, Mrs. Clemens did so.

Sam's hand came from his pocket and opened within hers.

A scream followed. "What is it? Oh, my heavens, it's a bat! Oh, you dreadful boy! Oh, the horrid thing!"

As Mrs. Clemens rushed to the window to fling away her present, Sam quickly skipped from the room.

Samuel Clemens, better known as Mark Twain

UNIT THREE

The Whole Chapter

Merlin in the Giant's Dungeon

from

THE SWORD IN THE STONE

by

T. H. WHITE

In *The Sword and the Stone,* T. H. White tells the story of the boyhood of the legendary King Arthur. "Merlin in the Giant's Dungeon" is just one of the many adventures that "the Wart" has with his teacher, Merlin the magician.

The boy Arthur, known as "the Wart," lay on the floor of the castle, staring into the fire. Merlin the Magician sat beside him. They were listening to old Sir Alfred read a story about a giant.

"Have you ever seen a giant?" Merlin asked the Wart softly, so as not to interrupt the reading.

"No," whispered the Wart. "But I'd like to."

"Just catch hold of my hands a moment," said Merlin. "And shut your eyes."

The Wart did as Merlin the Magician said. And at once he and Merlin were standing hand in hand in a forest.

"This is the forest of the giant Galapas," said Merlin. "And we are going to see him at his castle. Now listen. You are invisible at the moment because you are holding my hand. I can keep you invisible as long as you hold on to me. But if you let go of me, even for a moment, during that moment you will become visible. And, if you do in front of the giant Galapas, he will eat you up in two bites. So hold on."

"Very well," said the Wart.

"Don't say, 'Very well.' It isn't very well at all around here. It is very tricky indeed. The whole of the giant's forest is dotted with traps. So I shall thank you to look where you are going."

"What kind of traps?" asked the Wart.

"The giant Galapas digs holes about ten feet deep, with smooth walls, and covers them over with branches and grasses and such. Then, if people walk about, they fall into them. And he goes around every morning to finish them off and carry them home for dinner."

"Very well," said the Wart again. Then he caught himself. And quickly he changed his words to, "I will be careful."

Being invisible is not so nice as it sounds, the Wart soon found out. After a few minutes of it, he forgot where he last left his hands and legs.

Or he could only guess to within three or four inches. So it was by no means easy to make his way through the forest.

"Hold on," said Merlin. "And don't trip up."

With each step, the Wart stared at the ground in front of him, knowing it might give way into a deep hole. It was a while before he and Merlin came up to the wall around the giant's castle.

"Talk in whispers," said Merlin, "if you have to talk."

The wall in front of them had fruit trees along it. They climbed carefully, stepping on each other's backs and giving a hand up from on top. But every time the Wart had to let go of Merlin for a moment, he began to become visible. It was like an early movie, flashing off and on very badly. A gardener, looking at that part of the wall, tapped himself on the head and went away into a bush to be sick.

"Be very quiet now," whispered Merlin from the top of the wall. "There's Galapas." And they looked down upon the giant himself as he took his evening walk in the garden.

"But he's not big at all," whispered the Wart disappointedly.

"He is ten feet high," hissed Merlin. "And that is very big even for a giant. I picked the best one I knew.

The next biggest was only nine feet, four inches. If you don't like him, you can go home."

"I'm sorry. I didn't mean to sound disappointed, Merlin. Only I thought giants were sixty feet tall and that kind of thing."

"Sixty feet!" sniffed the magician.

The giant had heard something at the top of the wall. He looked up toward them but saw nothing, of course. "What strange noises!" he said to himself. "Bats, I suppose."

Merlin lowered his voice and explained, "People find big teeth and bones in the ground. And then they tell stories about giants. It's dragons, not giants, that grow really big."

"But can't people grow really big, too?" the Wart asked.

"I don't fully understand it myself, but it's something about people's bones," said Merlin. "If a man was to grow sixty feet high, he would snap his bones because they would be too heavy for his body."

"Well," said the Wart. "I must say it's rather a disappointment. I don't mean being brought to see him," he added quickly. "But it's that they don't grow like I thought. Still, I suppose ten feet is quite big when you come to think of it."

"Indeed it is," said Merlin. "You would not even come up to his belt. And he could throw you up in the air as high as you could throw a small table."

As they talked on, they forgot to be careful of their voices. And now the giant came toward them and stared hard at the wall on which they were sitting, invisible. "Noisy bats!" he said in an angry voice. And he turned and headed back into his castle.

"Follow him," whispered Merlin.

Quickly they climbed down from the wall, joined hands, and hurried after the giant.

They followed him into his dungeon. Here drops of water ran down dirty walls. Messages were written on the stone. One said, "Oh, if only I had paid for my dog's blanket, I should never have come to this pass." Another said, "How I wish I had not forgotten to feed my poor bird. Now I am in the same fix." It was a frightening place.

"Now then!" cried the giant Galapas, stopping outside one of his cells. "What about your ransom money, you dirty pig?"

"I'm not a pig," said a voice from the cell. "And I'm not dirty. Or I wasn't until I fell into that pit in the forest. Now I've got grass and leaves all down my back. What have you done with my toothbrush, you giant?"

152

"Never mind your toothbrush," shouted Galapas. "What about that ransom?"

"I want to brush my teeth," said the man in the cell, moving forward.

Now the Wart could see that he was an old man, tall and thin, with white hair.

The man went on, "My teeth feel funny, if you understand what I mean. And it makes me feel not very well."

The Wart pulled at Merlin's hand. "That's old Sir Pellinore!" he whispered.

"Have you no finer feelings?" roared the giant.

"No," said Pellinore. "I don't think I have. I want to brush my teeth."

"Do you think of nothing but your teeth?" screamed Galapas.

"I think of lots of things, old boy," said Pellinore. "I think how nice it would be to have an egg for breakfast, what?"

"Well, you can't have an egg. You shall just stay there until you pay my ransom. How do you suppose I am to run my castle if I don't have my ransom money? Do you suppose that all this is run on nothing?" The giant threw up his hands and moved on to another cell.

"We shall have to save poor old Sir Pellinore,"

the Wart said to Merlin. "He must have fallen into one of those traps you were telling me about. He is always wandering around, looking for the Questing Beast."

Forgetting to whisper, the Wart had spoken loudly enough for the giant to hear.

"Who's there?" shouted the giant Galapas, wheeling around.

"It's nothing," cried Merlin. "Only a mouse."

The giant stared down the hall. "No," he said slowly. "Mice don't talk in words."

"Eeeek," said Merlin, hoping that this would do.

"You can't fool me," said Galapas. "Now I shall come after you. And I shall see what you are."

"Don't be silly," said Merlin. "It is only a mouse, or two mice. You ought to know better."

"It is an invisible magician," said Galapas. "And as for invisible magicians, I tear them apart, see. Now, where are you, magician, so that I may tear you apart?"

The Wart backed away. "Hold on," cried Merlin as he felt the boy's hand slip out of his.

"Aha! A visible magician now," said the giant. "But only a small one." He reached out for the Wart's neck.

But Merlin caught hold of the Wart's hand in time.

155

"Gone again," said Galapas, kicking at where they had been.

Merlin put his invisible mouth right up to the Wart's invisible ear. "Listen," he whispered. "I think I hear something coming."

Galapas heard it too. It was from outside, a kind of barking, coming closer.

Pellinore, who had been listening at his window while all this was going on, began to jump and hop. "It's it!" he shouted.

"What's it?" hissed the giant.

"It!" explained the old knight. "It, itself!"

The noise had come nearer, and now was just outside the dungeon door. The door gave way with a crash, and in leaped the Questing Beast.

"Let go of me," cried the giant, as the Questing Beast fixed its teeth into the seat of his pants. Galapas pulled free, dropping his keys as he ran.

Quickly the invisible Wart opened Pellinore's cell. Then he and Merlin slipped away and hurried back through the forest.

"Faster," said Merlin. "We're running out of time."

Thinking of all the things that had happened, the Wart decided that "time" was strange indeed. For when he opened his eyes he was back at the castle,

lying on the floor near the fire. Merlin was sitting beside him. And old Sir Alfred was still reading to them from the book about the giant.

 *   *   *   *

In other chapters in *The Sword in the Stone* Merlin changes the Wart into a fish, a bird, and a snake, so that he can learn the ways of all living things as he grows up to become the great King Arthur.

UNIT FOUR

Numbers, Nature, and Nonsense

What Lucy Found There

from

THE LION, THE WITCH AND THE WARDROBE

by

C. S. LEWIS

Once there were four children whose names were Peter, Susan, Edmund, and Lucy. This story is about something that happened to them when they were sent away from London during the war because of the air raids. They were sent to live with an old Professor who lived in the heart of the country.

Early one rainy morning, the children decided to explore the house. Lucy discovered a big wardrobe in an empty room. The door of the wardrobe opened easily, and she stepped inside. As she walked deeper and deeper into the wardrobe, she found herself in the middle of the woods with snow under her feet!

Lucy walked on toward a lamp-post, and a very strange person stepped out from among the trees into the light.

He was only a little taller than Lucy, and he carried an umbrella. From the waist up he was like a man, but his legs were shaped like a goat's. He was called a Faun. He carried several brown paper parcels. But when he saw Lucy, he was so surprised that he dropped all his parcels.

"Goodness gracious me!" exclaimed the Faun.

ood evening," said Lucy. But the Faun was
so busy picking up his parcels that at first he did not
reply. When he had finished he made her a little bow.

"Good evening, good evening," said the Faun.
"Excuse me—I don't want to be inquisitive—but
should I be right in thinking that you are a Daughter
of Eve?"

"My name's Lucy," said she, not quite understand-
ing him.

"But you are—forgive me—you are what they call a girl?" asked the Faun.

"Of course I'm a girl," said Lucy.

"You are in fact Human?"

"Of course I'm human," said Lucy, still a little puzzled.

"To be sure, to be sure," said the Faun. "How stupid of me! But I've never seen a Son of Adam or a Daughter of Eve before. I am delighted! That is to say—" and then he stopped as if he had been going to say something he had not intended but had remembered in time. "Delighted, delighted," he went on. "Allow me to introduce myself. My name is Tumnus."

"I am very pleased to meet you, Mr. Tumnus," said Lucy.

"And may I ask, O Lucy, Daughter of Eve," said Mr. Tumnus, "how you have come into Narnia?"

"Narnia? What's that?" said Lucy.

"This is the land of Narnia," said the Faun, "where we are now; all that lies between the lamp-post and the great castle of Cair Paravel on the eastern sea. And you—you have come from the wild woods of the west?"

"I—I got in through the wardrobe in the spare room," said Lucy.

"Ah!" said Mr. Tumnus in a rather melancholy voice, "if only I had worked harder at geography when I was a little Faun, I should no doubt know all about those strange countries. It is too late now."

"But they aren't countries at all," said Lucy, almost laughing. "It's only just back there—at least—I'm not sure. It is summer there."

"Meanwhile," said Mr. Tumnus, "it is winter in Narnia, and has been for ever so long, and we shall both catch cold if we stand here talking in the snow. Daughter of Eve from the far land of Spare Oom where eternal summer reigns around the bright city of War Drobe, how would it be if you came and had tea with me?"

"Thank you very much, Mr. Tumnus," said Lucy. "But I was wondering whether I ought to be getting back."

"It's only just round the corner," said the Faun, "and there'll be a roaring fire—and toast—and sardines—and cake."

"Well, it's very kind of you," said Lucy. "But I shan't be able to stay long."

"If you will take my arm, Daughter of Eve," said Mr. Tumnus, "I shall be able to hold the umbrella over both of us. That's the way. Now—off we go."

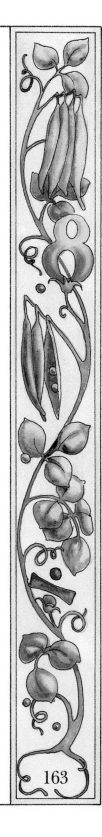

And so Lucy found herself walking through the wood arm in arm with this strange creature as if they had known one another all their lives.

They had not gone far before they came to a place where the ground became rough and there were rocks all about and little hills up and little hills down. At the bottom of one small valley Mr. Tumnus turned suddenly aside as if he were going to walk straight into an unusually large rock, but at the last moment Lucy found he was leading her into the entrance of a cave.

As soon as they were inside she found herself blinking in the light of a wood fire. Then Mr. Tumnus stooped and took a flaming piece of wood out of the fire with a neat little pair of tongs, and lit a lamp. "Now we shan't be long," he said, and immediately put a kettle on.

Lucy thought she had never been in a nicer place. It was a little, dry, clean cave of reddish stone with a carpet on the floor and two little chairs ("one for me and one for a friend," said Mr. Tumnus) and a table and a dresser and a mantelpiece over the fire and above that a picture of an old Faun with a grey beard. In one corner there was a door which Lucy thought must lead to Mr. Tumnus' bedroom, and on one wall was a shelf full of books. Lucy looked at

these while he was setting out the tea things. They
had titles like *The Life and Letters of Silenus* or *Nymphs
and Their Ways* or *Men, Monks and Gamekeepers; a Study
in Popular Legend* or *Is Man a Myth?*

"Now, Daughter of Eve!" said the Faun.

And really it was a wonderful tea. There was a nice
brown egg, lightly boiled, for each of them, and then
sardines on toast, and then buttered toast, and then
toast with honey, and then a sugar-topped cake. And
when Lucy was tired of eating the Faun began to talk.

He had wonderful tales to tell of life in the forest.
He told about the midnight dances and how the
Nymphs who lived in the wells and the Dryads who
lived in the trees came out to dance with the Fauns;
about long hunting parties after the milk-white
Stag who could give you wishes if you caught him;

165

about feasting and treasure-seeking with the wild
Red Dwarfs in deep mines and caverns far beneath
the forest floor; and then about summer when the
woods were green and old Silenus on his fat donkey
would come to visit them, and sometimes Bacchus
himself, and then the streams would run with wine
instead of water and the whole forest would give
itself up to jollification for weeks on end.

"Not that it isn't always winter now," he added
gloomily. Then to cheer himself up he took out from
its case on the dresser a strange little flute that looked
as if it were made of straw and began to play. And the
tune he played made Lucy want to cry and laugh and
dance and go to sleep all at the same time. It must
have been hours later when she shook herself and
said,

"Oh Mr. Tumnus—I'm so sorry to stop you, and I
do love that tune—but really, I must go home. I only
meant to stay for a few minutes."

"It's no good *now,* you know," said the Faun, laying
down his flute and shaking his head at her very
sorrowfully.

"No good?" said Lucy, jumping up and feeling
rather frightened. "What do you mean? I've got to
go home at once. The others will be wondering what
has happened to me." But a moment later she asked,

"Mr. Tumnus! Whatever is the matter?" for the Faun's brown eyes had filled with tears and then the tears began trickling down his cheeks, and soon they were running off the end of his nose; and at last he covered his face with his hands and began to howl.

"Mr. Tumnus! Mr. Tumnus!" said Lucy in great distress. "Don't! Don't! What is the matter? Aren't you well? Dear Mr. Tumnus, do tell me what is wrong." But the Faun continued sobbing as if his heart would break.

And even when Lucy went over and put her arms round him and lent him her handkerchief, he did not stop. He merely took the handkerchief and kept on using it, wringing it out with both hands whenever it got too wet to be any more use, so that presently Lucy was standing in a damp patch.

"Mr. Tumnus!" bawled Lucy in his ear, shaking him. "Do stop. Stop it at once! You ought to be ashamed of yourself, a great big Faun like you. What on earth are you crying about?"

"Oh—oh—oh!" sobbed Mr. Tumnus, "I'm crying because I'm such a bad Faun."

"I don't think you're a bad Faun at all," said Lucy. "I think you are a very good Faun. You are the nicest Faun I've ever met."

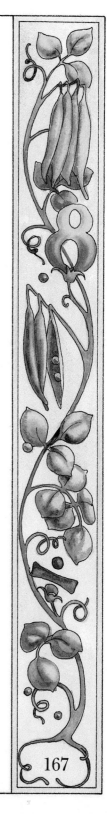

"Oh—oh—you wouldn't say that if you knew," replied Mr. Tumnus between his sobs. "No, I'm a bad Faun. I don't suppose there ever was a worse Faun since the beginning of the world."

"But what have you done?" asked Lucy.

"My old father, now," said Mr. Tumnus, "that's his picture over the mantelpiece. He would never have done a thing like this."

"A thing like what?" asked Lucy.

"Like what I've done," said the Faun. "Taken service under the White Witch. That's what I am. I'm in the pay of the White Witch."

"The White Witch? Who is she?"

"Why, it is she that has got all Narnia under her thumb. It's she that makes it always winter. Always winter and never Christmas; think of that!"

"How awful!" said Lucy. "But what does she pay *you* for?"

"That's the worst of it," said Mr. Tumnus with a deep groan. "I'm a kidnapper for her, that's what I am. Look at me, Daughter of Eve. Would you believe that I'm the sort of Faun to meet a poor innocent child in the wood, one that had never done me any harm, and pretend to be friendly with it, and invite it home to my cave, all for the sake of lulling it asleep and then handing it over to the White Witch?"

"No," said Lucy. "I'm sure you wouldn't do anything of the sort."

"But I have," said the Faun.

"Well," said Lucy rather slowly (for she wanted to be truthful and yet not be too hard on him), "well, that was pretty bad. But you're so sorry for it that I'm sure you will never do it again."

"Daughter of Eve, don't you understand?" said the Faun. "It isn't something I *have* done. I'm doing it now, this very moment."

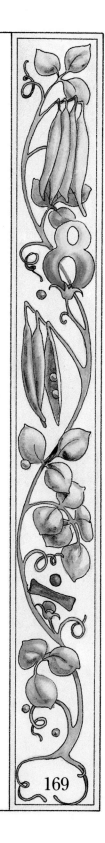

"What do you mean?" cried Lucy, turning white.

"You are the child," said Mr. Tumnus. "I had orders from the White Witch that if I ever saw a Son of Adam or a Daughter of Eve in the wood, I was to catch them and hand them over to her. And you are the first I ever met. And I've pretended to be your friend and asked you to tea, and all the time I've been meaning to wait till you were asleep and then go and tell *her.*"

"Oh but you won't, Mr. Tumnus," said Lucy. "You won't, will you? Indeed, indeed you really mustn't."

"And if I don't," said he, beginning to cry again, "she's sure to find out. And she'll have my tail cut off, and my horns sawn off, and my beard plucked out, and she'll wave her hand over my beautiful cloven hoofs and turn them into horrid solid hoofs like a wretched horse's. And if she is extra and specially angry she'll turn me into stone and I shall be only a statue of a Faun in her horrible house until the four thrones at Cair Paravel are filled—and goodness knows when that will happen, or whether it will ever happen at all."

"I'm very sorry, Mr. Tumnus," said Lucy. "But please let me go home."

"Of course I will," said the Faun. "Of course I've got to. I see that now. I hadn't known what Humans were like before I met you. Of course I can't give you up to the Witch; not now that I know you. But we must be off at once. I'll see you back to the lamp-post. I suppose you can find your own way from there back to Spare Oom and War Drobe?"

"I'm sure I can," said Lucy.

"We must go as quietly as we can," said Mr. Tumnus. "The whole wood is full of *her* spies. Even some of the trees are on her side."

They both got up and left the tea things on the table, and Mr. Tumnus once more put up his umbrella and gave Lucy his arm, and they went out into the snow. The journey back was not at all like the journey to the Faun's cave; they stole along as quickly as they could, without speaking a word, and Mr. Tumnus kept to the darkest places. Lucy was relieved when they reached the lamp-post again.

"Do you know your way from here, Daughter of Eve?" said Tumnus.

Lucy looked very hard between the trees and could just see in the distance a patch of light that looked like daylight. "Yes," she said, "I can see the wardrobe door."

"Then be off home as quick as you can," said the Faun, "and—c-can you ever forgive me for what I meant to do?"

"Why, of course I can," said Lucy, shaking him heartily by the hand. "And I do hope you won't get into dreadful trouble on my account."

171

"Farewell, Daughter of Eve," said he. "Perhaps I may keep the handkerchief?"

"Rather!" said Lucy, and then ran towards the far-off patch of daylight as quickly as her legs would carry her. And presently instead of rough branches brushing past her she felt coats, and instead of crunching snow under her feet she felt wooden boards, and all at once she found herself jumping out of the wardrobe into the same empty room from which the whole adventure had started.

She shut the wardrobe door tightly behind her and looked around, panting for breath. It was still raining and she could hear the voices of the others in the passage.

"I'm here," she shouted. "I'm here. I've come back, I'm all right."

♦   ♦   ♦   ♦

Soon all the children enter the wardrobe and discover Lucy's strange and exciting world. They help the creatures and their lion-king, Aslan, fight against the White Witch and free Narnia from her evil spell.

Read more about the children's adventures in *The Lion, the Witch and the Wardrobe* by C. S. Lewis.

How the Clever Doctor Tricked Death

a Hispanic tale from the Dominican Republic retold by

DOROTHY SHARP CARTER

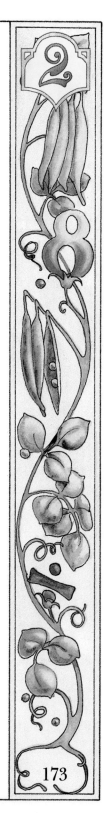

There was once a very rough fellow who always had a fine idea trickling through his head: once I find work I am sure to become rich quickly. He had faith. The desire to search for work he had not.

One day Death stood before him. "Fellow, I have taken a fancy to you. Such a strong fancy that I will look out for you. Now heed me. You shall take the profession of doctor. As *médico* you will be able to cure anyone on whom you lay your hand—on these conditions. If you see me standing at the foot of the sick one's bed you may cure him at once. But, if you see me at the *head* of the bed, do not trouble yourself. Go for a walk. Play some chess. Sip a cup of coffee. There is no cure, and he is mine."

The fellow went off to the city and began to practice medicine. *His* type of medicine. Not a bad type either. After a time he had cured dozens—hundreds—thousands of patients. Soon there ran through the town a rumor that a doctor lived therein who could accomplish miracles.

The rumor, after many twists and turns and rushing into blind alleys, finally reached the palace. Here it was welcomed by the King, who had a daughter, gravely ill. At once he sent for the doctor.

As soon as this one arrived breathless (one doesn't skimp on breath at a king's summons), the King spoke. "The princess is ill. Seriously ill. If you save her you shall have half my kingdom. And marry the princess in the bargain. On the other hand, if you allow her to die—off comes your head."

Rather unfair of the King. He gave the doctor no choice at all. So you can imagine what choice the doctor *did* make. He agreed. Oh, heartily. Anyway, he was convinced he could cure the girl. No problem. He was so accustomed to seeing Death at the foot of the bed, the old rascal might have been a bedpost.

But *this* time—lo and behold, Death stood big as life at the *head* of the bed. It gave the doctor quite a turn. Ay, he said to himself, instead of curing her and living like a king, am I to die? Are we both to die? *Ay*, what to do? *Ay, ay, ay.* . . .

Then an idea came. Swiftly he seized the bed and yanked it around foot to wall instead of head to wall.

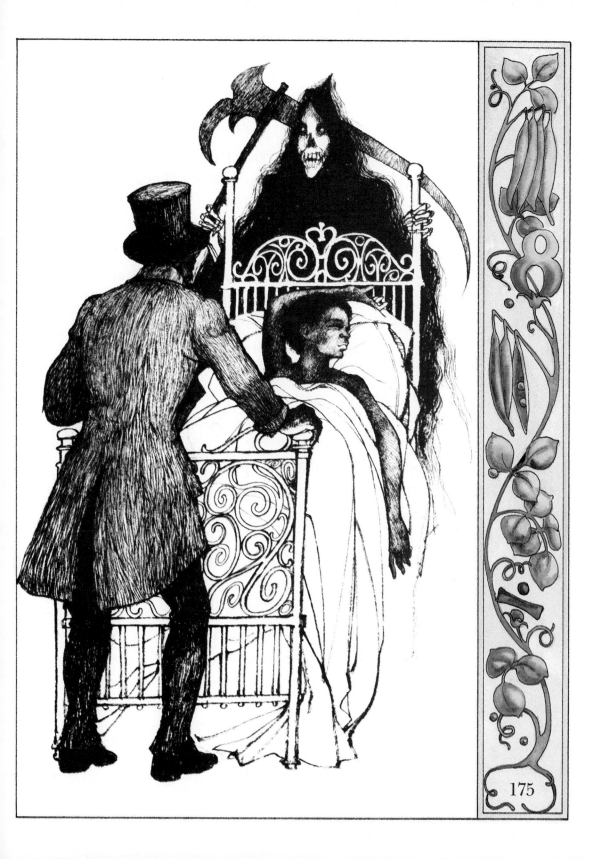

And Death suddenly found himself at the foot of the bed—watching the doctor assist the cured princess to sit up. Wasn't he put out! Furious. He sallied out the door swearing revenge on the clever doctor.

At least the King kept his promise. (They sometimes don't, you know.) He made the arrangement for handing over half his riches and also set the date for the wedding. After all, it's rather nice to have a doctor in the family, particularly a good one.

However, when the doctor left the palace, who should catch his sleeve but—Death. "Come with me," he commanded.

Before he knew it the doctor was up in the sky, standing on a heavenly blue carpet. And around him were hundreds—thousands—millions of little oil lamps.

"See you these lamps?" asked Death sternly. "Each one is the life of someone on earth. When the oil is gone so is the life. Here is yours—this with only a dab of wetness in the bottom. Five minutes of flame. Five minutes of life, my clever doctor."

"Very well." The doctor sighed. "But add enough oil to last fifteen minutes and I shall tell you a story. One of my best. . . ."

He watched to see where Death dipped out a centigram of oil. Then while he told his story, though it was a good one, Death dozed, and the doctor refueled his lamp . . . to the very top and dribbling over. So that even today he still lives. I know, for he is an old acquaintance of mine. He it is who told me this tale.

177

Limericks

by

EDWARD LEAR

There was a young lady whose chin
Resembled the point of a pin.
    So she had it made sharp
    And purchased a harp,
And played several tunes with her chin.

There was an old man who said, "Well!
Will nobody answer this bell?
    I have pulled day and night,
    Till my hair has grown white,
But nobody answers this bell!"

There was an old person of Dean
Who dined on one pea and one bean.
    For he said, "More than that
    Would make me too fat!"
That cautious old person of Dean.

W's for Windows

by

PHYLLIS McGINLEY

W's for Windows.
    Watch them welcome in the night.
How they twinkle, twinkle, twinkle
    With the waning of the light!
There's nothing half so wonderful
    In all the wond'rous town
As a million winking Windows
    When the dusk is coming down.

W

by

JAMES REEVES

The King sent for his wise men all
  To find a rhyme for W.
When they had thought a good long time
But could not think of a single rhyme,
"I'm sorry," said he, "to trouble you."

181

The Islands of Circe and the Sirens

from the

ODYSSEY

by

HOMER

Long ago there was a city named Troy that had a strong wall around it for defense. During the great Trojan War, the Greeks tricked the Trojans into opening the gate of their wall to pull in a huge wooden horse.

The Trojans thought the horse was a gift. But it was really a hollow hiding place for Greek warriors. Once inside the city, those warriors beat the Trojans. Then the Greeks were ready to sail back home as victorious heroes.

It took years for the hero named Ulysses to reach home because he had so many adventures along the way. Writers have been retelling the adventures of Ulysses for thousands of years.

After Ulysses and his men escaped from the cave of the one-eyed giant, they sailed away from the island of the Cyclopes. From there, the winds blew them to the island where Circe, daughter of the sun, lived.

Circe's enchantments were strong and strange. Men who fell under her spell never left her island.

But Ulysses and his men did not know what was in store for them when they were blown her way.

After landing on her shore, Ulysses climbed a hill. Looking about, he could see no signs of life except in one spot in the middle of the island. There he saw a castle.

Ulysses ordered half of his men to go to the castle and see if they were welcomed. As the men neared the castle, they found themselves followed by lions, foxes, and wolves. But these animals did not seem wild, and the men looked at them in wonder.

Now these animals had once been men, and had been changed by Circe's magic into animals. Circe changed proud men into lions and sly men into foxes and mean men into wolves.

When Ulysses's men reached the castle, they could hear music, and the breezes carried the good smell of food cooking. Circe herself came forth and invited them in for a feast.

All but one of the men were quick to accept her invitation. That man decided to hide himself in a tall tree where he could watch and see what happened.

"Eat well," said Circe as she led them to her table. "Drink as much as you wish." She kept their cups full. Course after course of food was set before them, each more tasty than the one before. The men ate like pigs, not stopping even when they were stuffed.

Then Circe reached out her hand, and as she touched each man, he turned into a pig. Their bodies only were changed. They kept their minds. Then she shut them up in pigpens and gave them garbage to eat.

The man who had watched climbed down from the tree and ran back to the ship to tell Ulysses what he had seen.

"She must set my men free from this enchantment!" cried Ulysses upon hearing that Circe had turned his men into pigs. "I will go to her myself. I will find a way to make her change them back into men."

On his way to the castle, he met a young man who seemed to know all about him. This man told Ulysses, "I am Mercury, messenger of the gods. I have come to tell you how to protect yourself against Circe's magic."

He gave Ulysses some leaves of a plant. "Chew these leaves," said Mercury. "They will enable you to keep your form as a man, even when she uses her enchantments upon you."

Ulysses thanked him, chewed the leaves, and went on toward the castle. When he arrived, Circe invited him in and gave him food and drink, just as she had done for his men.

185

When he was full, she touched him, saying, "Be changed. You will no longer walk on two legs but on four. You will go into the pigpen with your friends."

But instead of turning into a pig, he pulled out his sword and pointed it at her. "Set my men free, or die!" he cried.

Circe fell to her knees, for she knew she was facing a hero who had special help from the gods. "I will lift my enchantment," she promised, "and your men will walk upright again."

At once she changed the pigs back into men. Ulysses was so pleased that he stayed on her island for a long time, but finally his friends made him see that he must try again to get home.

Sadly Circe saw him to his ship. "When you sail from here, you must plug your ears to get past the Sirens," she told him.

"Why?" said Ulysses. "Who are the Sirens?"

"The Sirens are maids of the sea who sit on rocks and sing so sweetly that sailors are irresistibly drawn to them. Many a ship has sailed too close and then crashed on their rocks, and many a man has thrown himself into the sea and tried to swim to them."

"I would greatly like to hear the song of the Sirens," said Ulysses.

Circe smiled sadly. "You cannot hear it and live, for

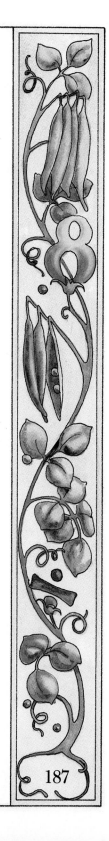

the Sirens will draw you to them, and you will be dashed against the rocks."

"Not I," said Ulysses. "I would not be such a fool."

Circe thought for a moment. "Perhaps there is a way," she said. Then she told Ulysses to plug the ears of his men so that they could not hear the Sirens and to have himself tied to the mast with heavy ropes.

"Tell your men," she went on, "that even if you order them to untie you, they must not let you loose. Only after you have passed the Sirens and can hear their songs no longer—only then will it be safe to set you free."

Ulysses did as she said.

As his ship neared the island of the Sirens, he heard music so lovely that he wanted to throw himself into the water and swim to the singers. Ulysses struggled and twisted against his ropes.

He shouted at his men, "Untie me! Let me loose!"

But their ears were plugged. They heard neither his shouts nor the songs of the Sirens. True to his orders, they held the ship on course and sailed on. Only when the Sirens were out of sight and out of hearing did the men set Ulysses free.

A Bad Singer

by

SAMUEL TAYLOR COLERIDGE

Swans sing before they die—
'Twere no bad thing
Should certain persons die
Before they sing.

Rip Van Winkle

by

WASHINGTON IRVING

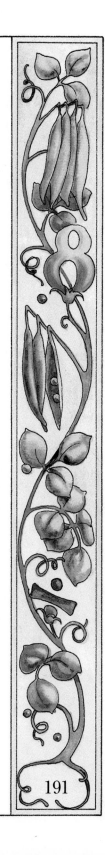

Whoever has made a voyage up the Hudson River must remember the Kaatskill Mountains. At the foot of these mountains a traveler can still see light smoke curling up from the chimneys of some old houses in a little village.

In that same village, and in one of those very houses, there once lived a fellow named Rip Van Winkle.

He was a simple, easygoing man who liked to hunt and fish, but did not like to labor on his farm. He was also a good neighbor, and a henpecked husband who patiently endured his wife's shrill nagging without ever answering back.

Indeed, the patience and meekness he learned at home made him popular with everyone. If a nagging wife may, therefore, be thought of as a blessing, Rip Van Winkle was greatly blessed.

He was friendly with all the men of the village.

191

He was even willing to run errands for their wives. These good wives, of course, took Rip's part in all his family squabbles. They never failed, when they gossiped about these matters, to lay all the blame on Rip's wife, Dame Van Winkle, and her sharp tongue.

The children of the village would shout with joy when Rip approached. He taught them to fly kites and shoot marbles. Sometimes he told them long stories of ghosts, witches, and Indians.

Indeed, Rip was always ready to help with anybody's business except his own. But as to doing family duty and keeping his own farm in order, he found it impossible. His fences were always falling to pieces. He daydreamed and let his cow go astray. His fields were overgrown with weeds.

His children, too, were as ragged and wild as if they belonged to nobody. His young son Rip seemed to be growing more and more like his father, taking on his idle habits as well as his old clothes.

If left to himself, Rip Van Winkle would have whistled life away in great contentment. But morning, noon, and night, his wife kept up her nagging. She went on and on about his laziness and the ruin he was bringing upon his family.

Rip had but one way of replying to her lectures. He shrugged his shoulders, shook his head, cast up his eyes, but said nothing. As soon as he could, he would take to the outside of the house—the only side which, in truth, belongs to a henpecked husband.

For a long while, when driven from home, Rip would join other idle men of the village on the benches in front of a small inn. Here they would sit in the shade through a long lazy summer's day, talking over village gossip or telling endless sleepy stories about nothing. But even here, Rip's wife felt free to break in upon the gathering and charge all the men with laziness.

At last poor Rip was reduced almost to despair. He had only one way left to escape from the labor of his farm and the clamor of his wife. It was to stroll into the woods, with his hunting dog Wolf at his side and his gun in hand, saying he would bring back some game for dinner.

One day, on a long ramble of this kind, Rip climbed to the highest parts of the Kaatskill Mountains. On one side he saw the Hudson River, far below him. On the other side he looked down into a deep valley, wild and lonely.

For some time, Rip gazed at the scene. Evening came on, and the mountains began to throw long blue shadows over the valley.

As he started down, he heard a voice from a

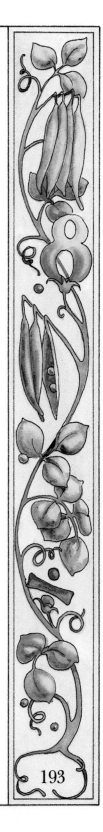

distance calling, "Rip Van Winkle! Rip Van Winkle!"

He looked around, but he could see no one.

Rip turned again to descend when he heard the same cry ring through the still evening air.

"Rip Van Winkle! Rip Van Winkle!"

At the same time, his dog Wolf shivered, gave a low growl, and pressed against his master's side.

Rip now felt the beginnings of fear stealing over him. As he peered down, he could just make out the figure of a short, square-built fellow, carrying a keg on his shoulder.

The fellow made signs for Rip to approach and help him with the load. He was strangely dressed, with a high-crowned hat and feather.

Though puzzled and somewhat fearful, Rip did as he was told. As they walked together on the dry bed of a river, Rip every now and then heard long rolls of distant thunder.

At length they came to a flat spot where a group of bearded men were playing ninepins. They were all dressed in clothing of long ago, like Rip's guide.

Though it was clear that these folks were at play, they were strangely silent. Nothing broke the still-ness of the scene but the noise of the balls which, whenever they were rolled, echoed through the mountains like thunder.

Rip's guide made signs to him to draw drinks from the keg and serve the group. He obeyed with fear and trembling. They drank in silence and returned to their game.

Little by little, Rip felt less fearful. When no eye was upon him he even dared to taste their drink. One taste led to another until the drinks made him drowsy. His eyes swam in his head, and he fell into a deep sleep.

On waking he found himself on the mountaintop from which he had first seen the old man with the keg. He rubbed his eyes. It was a bright sunny morning. The birds were hopping among the bushes and singing.

"Surely," thought Rip, "I have not slept here all night." He recalled what had happened before he fell asleep. "Oh, what shall I say to Dame Van Winkle!"

He looked around for his gun. In place of the clean, well-oiled piece that he had been carrying, he found a rusty old gun lying by him. He now suspected that the silent players of last night had robbed him of his gun.

Wolf, too, had disappeared, but he might have strayed away after a squirrel. Rip whistled for his dog. Then he shouted, "Wolf!" The echoes repeated his whistle and his shout. But no dog was to be seen.

He decided to revisit the scene of last night. He would demand the return of his dog and his gun.

As he rose to walk, he found himself stiff in the joints. "These mountain beds do not agree with me," thought Rip. "And if this ramble should lay me up with a stiff back, what a time I shall have from Dame Van Winkle!"

With some trouble he got down to the place where he had met his guide of last night. Rip looked for the dry river bed where they had walked together.

But to his surprise a mountain stream was now foaming in it. He followed the stream, hoping it would lead him to the flat spot where the men had been playing ninepins. But no traces of such a spot were to be found. Poor Rip was brought to a standstill.

What was to be done? The morning was passing away, and Rip felt faint for the want of his breakfast. He grieved to give up his dog and gun. He dreaded to meet his wife. But it would not do to starve in the mountains. He shook his head, and with a heart full of trouble turned his steps homeward.

As Rip approached the village, he met a number of people, but none that he knew. This somewhat surprised him for he had thought he knew most of the people in the country round. Their dress, too,

197

looked different from what he usually saw on his neighbors.

They all stared at him with equal marks of surprise. Many stroked their chins when they gazed upon him. When Rip did the same, he found that his beard had grown a foot long.

He had now entered the village. A troop of strange children ran at his heels, pointing at his long gray beard. Dogs barked at him as he passed.

The very village was different. It was larger. There were rows of houses that he had never seen before. Strange names were over the doors. Strange faces were at the windows. Everything was strange.

Rip began to think maybe he and the world around him were bewitched. Surely this was his native village which he had left but the day before. There stood the Kaatskill Mountains. There ran the Hudson River. "Last night," thought he, "has mixed up my poor head sadly."

He had trouble finding the way to his own house, which he approached with fear in his heart. He expected any moment to hear the shrill voice of Dame Van Winkle. But the house had gone to ruin. The roof had fallen in, and the door was hanging off its hinges.

He entered the house, which, to tell the truth,

Dame Van Winkle had always kept in neat order. It was empty. Rip called loudly for his wife and children. The walls rang for a moment with his voice. Then all again was silence.

He now hurried forth to his old meeting place, the benches in front of the inn, looking for his friends and neighbors. There was, as usual, a crowd about the door, but no one that Rip remembered.

A man in a cocked hat asked him what he wanted.

Rip said he was in search of some of his neighbors.

"Well, who are they?" asked the man. "Name them."

Rip named one after another of the men who had passed afternoons with him here. He was told that one had been dead eighteen years. Another had moved away long ago. Still another had gone off to war and never come back.

Rip's heart died away at hearing of these sad changes in his home and friends and finding himself so alone in the world. He had no further courage to ask about any more of the people he had known. At last he cried out in despair, "Does nobody here know Rip Van Winkle?"

"Oh, Rip Van Winkle!" exclaimed two or three.

"Oh, to be sure! That's Rip Van Winkle yonder, leaning against the tree."

Rip turned his head and beheld a man who looked just like him, seemingly as lazy and certainly as ragged. He was now undone, wondering whether he was himself or that other fellow.

Then the man in the cocked hat demanded to know who he was and what was his name.

"I'm not myself," exclaimed Rip. "I'm somebody else. That's me yonder—no—that's somebody else got into my shoes. I was myself last night, but I fell asleep on the mountain, and they've changed my gun and everything's changed. And I'm changed, and I can't tell what's my name, or who I am!"

At this moment a young woman with a child in her arms joined the crowd. She made her way forward to get a look at the bearded man. The child, frightened at his looks, began to cry.

"Hush, Rip," said she. "Hush, the old man won't hurt you."

The tone of her voice awakened a train of memory in his mind. "What is your name, my good woman?" he asked.

"Judith Gardenier."

"And your father's name?"

"Ah, poor man! Rip Van Winkle was his name.

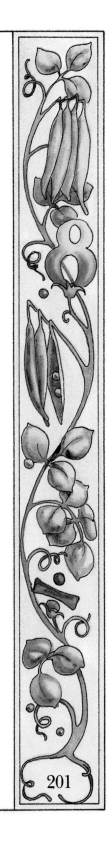

But it's twenty years since he went away from home with his gun and has never been heard of since. His dog came home without him. But whether he shot himself or was carried away by the Indians, nobody can tell. I was then but a little girl."

Rip had but one question more to ask. He asked it with a shaking voice. "Where is your mother?"

"Oh, she too died when I was younger. She broke a blood vessel in a fit of temper."

There was a drop of comfort, at least, in this.

The honest man could contain himself no longer. He caught his daughter and her child in his arms. "I am your father!" cried he. "Young Rip Van Winkle once, old Rip Van Winkle now! Does nobody know poor Rip Van Winkle?"

All stood amazed.

Then an old woman came forth, peered at his face for a moment, and said, "Sure enough! It is Rip Van Winkle! It is himself! Welcome home again, old neighbor. Where have you been these twenty long years?"

Rip's story was soon told, for the whole twenty years had been to him as one night. The neighbors stared when they heard it. Some were seen to wink at each other, and put their tongues in their cheeks. Others just shook their heads.

It was decided to take the opinion of old Peter Vanderdonk, who was in the crowd. Peter was the oldest man in the village, and knew well all of the strange happenings of the neighborhood. He remembered Rip at once, and nodded when he heard Rip's story.

Peter assured everyone that the Kaatskill Mountains had long been haunted by strange beings. He said it was a fact that the ghost of the great Hendrick Hudson, who had discovered the river and county, came back every twenty years with his crew. Peter claimed that his own father, like Rip Van Winkle, had once seen those men in their old Dutch clothing, playing ninepins in the mountains.

So, the crowd broke up and returned to other concerns. Rip's daughter took him home to live with her and the farmer she had married. As to Rip's son, who looked just like his father, he was hired by the daughter's husband as a farmhand. But like his father, he spent more time hunting and fishing than laboring on the farm.

Rip now took up his old walks and habits. He made friends among the new generation, with whom he grew into great favor as he told his story again and again to every child in the village.

Even to this day, some of those children's children never hear a thunderstorm in the Kaatskill Mountains but they say Hendrick Hudson and his crew are at their game of ninepins. And it is a common wish of all henpecked husbands in the neighborhood, when life hangs heavy on their hands, that they might have a quieting sip of Rip Van Winkle's drink.

Nothing New Under the Sun (Hardly)

from

HOMER PRICE

by

ROBERT McCLOSKEY

round noon, the talk in the Centerburg Barbershop had slowed down to nothing at all. The sheriff, the barber, and Homer Price's uncle were just looking out the window. A few children came into sight.

"School's out for lunch," said the sheriff.

Then the door opened and Homer came in.

"Hello, everybody," he said. "Uncle Ulysses, Aunt Aggy sent me to tell you to stir yourself over to the lunchroom and help serve blue-plate specials."

Uncle Ulysses sighed and prepared to leave, but before he got to the door, there was a noise outside.

The sheriff cupped a hand behind his ear. "What's that noise?" he said.

Everyone listened.

The noise (it was sort of a rattle) grew louder, and then suddenly an old car swung into the town square. The sheriff, the barber, Uncle Ulysses, and Homer watched it with open mouths as it rattled around the town square—once—twice—three times. On the third time, it slowed down and stopped right out front of Uncle Ulysses' lunchroom.

Everyone kept on staring, and it wasn't just because this car was old, much older than Homer. It wasn't because some strange business was built onto it, or that the strange business was covered with a large canvas. No. That wasn't what made Homer and the sheriff and Uncle Ulysses and the barber stare so long. It was the car's *driver.*

"Gosh, what a beard!" said Homer.

"And what a head of hair!" said the barber.

"Could you see his face?" asked the sheriff.

"Nope," answered Uncle Ulysses, still staring across the square.

They watched the stranger untangle his beard from the steering wheel and go into the lunchroom.

Uncle Ulysses promptly dashed for the door, saying, "See you later."

"Wait for me!" the sheriff called, "I'm sort of hungry."

Homer followed and the barber shouted, "Don't forget to come back and tell me the news!"

"O.K., and if I bring you a new customer I get a commission."

The stranger was sitting at the far end of the lunch counter, looking very shy and embarrassed. Homer's Aunt Aggy had already served him a blue-plate special and was eyeing him with suspicion. To be polite, Homer and Uncle Ulysses pretended to be busy behind the counter, and the sheriff pretended to study the menu—though he knew every single word on it by heart. They just glanced in the stranger's direction once in a while.

Finally Uncle Ulysses' curiosity got the best of him and he sauntered down to the stranger and asked, "Are you enjoying your lunch? Is everything all right?"

The stranger appeared to be very embarrassed, and you could easily tell that he was blushing underneath

his beard and all his hair. "Yes, sir, it's a very good lunch," he replied with a nod. When he nodded a stray whisp of beard accidentally got into the gravy. This made him more embarrassed than ever.

Uncle Ulysses waited for the stranger to start a conversation, but he didn't.

So Uncle Ulysses said, "Nice day today."

The stranger said, "Yes, nice day," and dropped a fork. Now the stranger *really* was embarrassed. He looked as though he would like to sink right through the floor.

Uncle Ulysses quickly handed the man another fork, and eased himself away, so as not to embarrass him into breaking a plate or falling off his stool.

After he finished lunch, the stranger reached into the pocket of his ragged, patched coat and drew out a leather moneybag. He paid for his lunch, nodded good-by, and crept out of the door and down the street with everyone staring after him.

Aunt Aggy broke the silence by bouncing on the marble counter the coin she had just received.

"It's good money," she pronounced, "but it looks as though it had been *buried* for *years!*"

"Shyest man I ever laid eyes on!" said Uncle Ulysses.

"Yes!" said the sheriff. "My as a shouse, I mean shy as a mouse!"

"Gosh, what a beard!" said Homer.

"Humph!" said Aunt Aggy. "Homer, it's time you started back to school!"

By mid-afternoon every man, woman, and child in Centerburg had something to gossip about, speculate on, and argue about.

Who was this stranger? Where did he come from?

Where was he going? How long was his beard, and his hair? What was his name? Did he have a business? What could be on the back of his car that was so carefully covered with the large canvas?

Nobody knew. Nobody knew anything about the stranger except that he parked his car in the town parking space and was spending considerable time walking about town. People reported that he paused in his walking and whistled a few bars of some strange tune, a tune nobody had ever heard of. The stranger was shy when grown-ups were near, and he would cross the street or go around a block to avoid speaking to someone. However, he did not avoid children. He smiled at them and seemed delighted to have them follow him.

People from all over town telephoned the sheriff at the barbershop asking about the stranger and making reports as to what was going on.

The sheriff was becoming a bit uneasy about the whole thing. He couldn't get near enough to the stranger to ask him his intentions, and if he *did* ask the stranger would be too shy to give him an answer.

As Homer passed by the barbershop on his way home from school the sheriff called him in. "Homer," he said, "I'm gonna need your help. This stranger with the beard has got me worried. You see, Homer, I can't find out who he is or what he is doing here in town. He's probably a nice enough fellow, just an individualist. But, then again, he might be a fugitive in disguise or something." Homer nodded. And the sheriff continued, "Now, what I want you to do is gain his confidence. He doesn't seem to be afraid of children, and you might be able to find out what this is all about. I'll treat you to a double raspberry sundae."

"It's a deal, sheriff!" said Homer. "I'll start right now."

At six o'clock Homer reported to the sheriff. "The stranger seems like a nice person, Sheriff," Homer began. "I walked down Market Street with him. He wouldn't tell me who he is or what he's doing, but he did say he'd been away from people for a great many years. He asked me to recommend a place for him to stay, and I said the Strand Hotel, so that's where he went just now when I left him. I'll have to run home

for dinner now, Sheriff, but I'll find out some more tomorrow. Don't forget about that raspberry sundae," said Homer.

"I won't," replied the sheriff, "and, Homer, don't forget to keep me posted on this fellow."

After Homer had gone, the sheriff turned to the barber and said, "Goll durnitt! We don't know one blessed thing about this fellow except that he's shy, and he's been away from people for quite a spell. For all we know he might be a fugitive, or a lunatic, or maybe one of these amnesia cases."

"If he didn't have so much hair I could tell in a second what kind of fellow he is," complained the sheriff. "Yep! Just one look at a person's ears and *I* can *tell!*"

"Well," said the barber, "*I* judge people by their *hair,* and I've been thinking. This fellow looks like somebody I've heard about, or read about somewhere. Like somebody out of a book, you understand, Sheriff?"

"Well, yes, in a way, but I could tell you definite with a good look at his ears!" said the sheriff. "Here comes Ulysses, let's ask him what *he* thinks."

Uncle Ulysses considered a second and said, "Well, *I* judge a person by his *waistline* and his *appetite.* Now I'm not saying I'm right, Sheriff, because I couldn't tell about his waistline under the old coat, but judging from his appetite I'd say he's a sort of person that I've read about somewhere. I can't just put my finger on it. Seems as though it must have been in a book."

"U-m-m," said the sheriff.

Just then Tony the shoe repairman came in for a haircut. After he was settled in the barber chair, the sheriff asked him what he thought about the mysterious stranger.

"Well, Sheriff, *I* judge everybody by their *feet* and their *shoes*. Nobody's worn a pair of gaiters like his for twenty-five years. It seems as though those shoes must have just up and walked right out of the pages of some old dusty book."

"There!" said the sheriff. "*Now* we're getting somewhere!"

He rushed to the phone and called Mr. Hirsh of the Hirsh Clothing Store, and asked, "Say, Sam, what do *you* think about this stranger? . . . Yes, the one bith the weard, I mean beard! . . . uh-huh . . . storybook clothes, eh? . . . Thanks a lot, Sam, good night."

Then he called the garage and said, "Hello, Luke, this is the sheriff talking. What do you make of this stranger in town . . . Yes? . . . literature, eh? Durn'd

if I kin see how you can judge a man by the car he drives, but I'll take your word for it. Good night, Luke, and thanks a lot."

The sheriff looked very pleased with himself. He paced up and down and muttered, "Getting somewhere! Getting somewhere at last!" Then he surprised everyone by announcing that he was going over to the *library!*

In a few minutes he was back, his mustache twitching with excitement. "I've solved it!" he shouted. "The librarian knew right off just what book to look in! It's *Rip Van Winkle!* It's Rip Van Winkle this fellow's like. He must have driven up into the hills some thirty years ago and fell asleep, or got amnesia, or something!"

"Yeah! That's it!" agreed the barber along with Uncle Ulysses and the shoemaker.

Then Uncle Ulysses asked, *"But* how about that 'whatever-it-is' underneath the canvas on the back of his car?"

"Now look here, Ulysses," shouted the sheriff, "you're just trying to complicate my deduction! Come on, let's play checkers!"

Bright and early the next morning the Rip-Van-Winklish stranger was up and wandering around Centerburg.

By ten o'clock everyone was referring to him as "Old Rip," and remarking how clever the sheriff was at deducting things.

The sheriff tried to see what was under the canvas, but couldn't make head or tail of what it was. Uncle Ulysses peeked at it too and said, "Goodness only knows! But never mind, Sheriff. If anybody can find out what this thing is, Homer will do the finding!"

That same afternoon after school was dismissed Uncle Ulysses and the sheriff saw Homer strolling down the street with "Old Rip."

"Looks like he's explaining something to Homer," said the sheriff.

"Homer'll find out!" said Uncle Ulysses proudly. Then they watched through the barbershop window while the stranger took Homer across the square to the parking lot and showed him his car. He lifted one corner of the canvas and pointed underneath, while Homer looked and nodded his head. They shook hands and the stranger went to his hotel, and Homer headed for the barbershop.

"Did he talk?" asked the sheriff the minute Homer opened the door.

"What's his name?" asked Uncle Ulysses.

"What is he doing?" asked the barber.

"Yes, he told me everything!" said Homer. "It sounds just like a story out of a book!"

"Yes, son, did he get amnesia up in the hills?" asked the sheriff.

"Well no, not exactly, Sheriff, but he did *live* in the hills for the past thirty years."

"Well, what's he doing here now?" the barber demanded.

"I better start at the beginning," said Homer.

"That's a good idea, son," said the sheriff. "I'll take a few notes just for future reference."

"Well, to begin with," Homer stated, "his name is Michael Murphy—just plain Michael Murphy. About thirty years ago he built himself a small vacation cabin out in the hills, some place on the far side of the state forest reserve. Then, he liked living in the cabin so much he decided to live there all of the time. He packed his belongings on his car and moved out to the hills."

"He cided ta be a dermit?" asked the sheriff.

"Not exactly a *hermit*," Homer continued. "But yesterday was the first time that he came out of the hills and saw people for thirty years. That's why he's so shy."

"Then he's moving back to civilization," suggested Uncle Ulysses.

"That comes later," said Homer, "I've only told as far as twenty-nine years ago."

"Can't you skip a few years, son, and get to the point?" demanded the sheriff.

"Nope! Twenty-nine years ago," Homer repeated firmly, "Mr. Murphy read in an almanac that if a man can make a better mousetrap than anybody else, the world will beat a path to his house—even if it is way out in the hills.

"So-o-o he started making *mousetraps.*"

There was a pause, and then the sheriff said, "Will you repeat that again, son?"

"I said, Mr. Murphy started making *mousetraps.* He made good ones too—the very best—and when one of Mr. Murphy's traps caught a mouse, that was the end of that mouse for all time."

The sheriff forgot all about taking notes as Homer continued, "But nobody came to buy the traps. But that was just as well, you see, because twenty-eight years ago Mr. Murphy began to feel *sorry* for the mice. He came to realize that he would have to change his whole approach. He thought and thought, and finally he decided to build mousetraps that wouldn't hurt the mice.

"He spent the next fifteen years doing research on what was the pleasantest possible way for a mouse to be caught. He discovered that being caught to music pleased mice the most, even more than cheese. Then," said Homer, "Mr. Murphy set to work to make a *musical* mousetrap."

"That wouldn't hurt the mice?" inquired Uncle Ulysses.

"That wouldn't hurt the mice," Homer started. "It was a long, hard job too, because first he had to build an organ out of reeds that the mice liked the sound of, and then he had to compose a tune that the mice couldn't possibly resist. Then he incorporated it all into a mousetrap . . . "

"That wouldn't hurt the mice?" interrupted the barber.

"That wouldn't hurt the mice," Homer went on. "The mousetrap caught mice, all right. The only trouble was, it was too big. What with the organ and all, and sort of impractical for general use because somebody had to stay around and pump the organ."

"Yes, I can see that wouldn't be practical," said Uncle Ulysses, stroking his chin—"but with a small electric motor . . . "

"But he solved it, Uncle Ulysses! The whole idea seems very practical after you get used to it. He decided since the trap was too large to use in a house, he would fasten it onto his car, which he

hadn't used for so long anyway. Then he could drive
it to a town and make a bargain with the mayor to
remove all the mice. You see he would start the
musical mousetrap to working, drive up and down
the streets and alleys. Then all of the mice would
run out of the houses to get themselves caught in
this trap that plays music that no mouse ever born
can possibly resist. After the trap is full of mice, Mr.
Murphy drives them out past the city limits,
somewhere where they can't find their way home,
and lets them go."

"Still without hurting them?" suggested the
barber.

"Of course," said Homer.

The sheriff chewed on his pencil, Uncle Ulysses
stroked on his chin, and the barber ran his fingers
through his hair.

Homer noticed the silence and said, "I guess the
idea *is* sort of startling when you first hear about it.
But if a town has a water truck to sprinkle streets,
and a street-sweeping truck to remove dirt, why
shouldn't they, maybe, just hire Mr. Murphy's musical
mousetrap once in a while to remove mice?" Uncle
Ulysses stroked his chin again and then said, "By
gum! This man Murphy is a genius!"

"I told Mr. Murphy that *you* would understand,

Uncle Ulysses!" said Homer with a grin. "I told him the mayor was a friend of yours, and you could talk him into anything, even hiring a musical mousetrap."

"Whoever heard of a micical moostrap!" said the sheriff.

"That doesn't hurt the *mice!*" added the barber as Homer and Uncle Ulysses went off arm in arm to see the mayor.

It scarcely took Uncle Ulysses and Homer half an hour to convince the mayor that Mr. Murphy's musical mousetrap should be hired to rid Centerburg of mice. While Uncle Ulysses chatted on with the mayor, Homer dashed over to the hotel to fetch Mr. Murphy.

Homer came back with the bearded inventor and introduced him to the mayor and to Uncle Ulysses. The mayor opened a drawer of his desk and brought out a bag of jelly beans. "Have one," he said to Mr. Murphy, to sort of break the ice and make his shy visitor feel at home. Mr. Murphy relaxed and answered the mayor's questions without blushing too much.

"How do we know this *thing of a jig* of yours will do what you say it will?" asked the mayor.

Mr. Murphy just whistled a few bars *"Tum tidy ay dee"* and a couple of mice jumped right out of the mayor's desk!

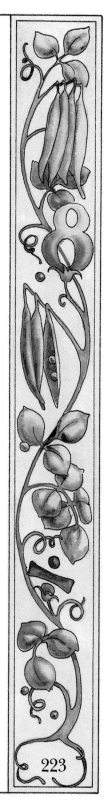

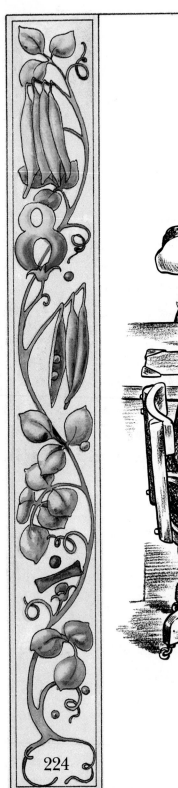

"Of course," Homer explained, "the mice come *quicker* and get *removed* when the mousetrap plays that tune through the streets. Mr. Murphy guarantees to remove every single mouse from Centerburg for only thirty dollars."

"It's a bargain!" said the mayor, "I wondered where my jelly beans were disappearing to!" and he shook hands with Mr. Murphy. Then he proclaimed Saturday as the day for demousing Centerburg. By this time everyone knew that the shy stranger's name was Michael Murphy, but people still spoke of him as Rip Van Winkle (Rip for short), because of the sheriff's deduction. Everybody talked about the musical mousetrap (that didn't hurt the mice) and the mayor's demousing proclamation.

The children, especially, were looking forward to the great event. They watched with interest while Mr. Murphy went over his car and his musical trap to be sure everything was in perfect working order. Homer and Freddy and most of the other children were planning to follow the trap all around town Saturday, and see the mice come out and get caught in Michael Murphy's musical trap.

"Gosh, Homer," said Freddy, "let's follow him until he lets them loose out in the country! That *will* be a sight, seeing all those mice let loose at once!"

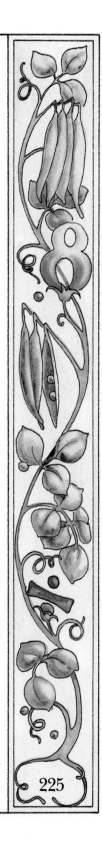

"Well, Freddy, I've been thinking it might not be a good idea to follow the mousetrap past the city limits," said Homer to Freddy's surprise.

"You know, Freddy, I've been over at the library reading up on mice and music—music can do funny things sometimes. It can soothe savage beasts and charm snakes and *lots* of things. If we're going to follow this musical trap till the mice are let loose, we better make some plans."

Homer and Freddy spent all Friday recess period making plans. They decided that all the children should meet in the school yard before the demousing started on Saturday. They arranged a signal, thumbs up, if everything was going along all right, and thumbs down if anyone was in trouble.

"It's just to be on the safe side," Homer explained.

Saturday dawned a beautiful crisp fall day, fine weather for the grand demousing of Centerburg. Mr. Michael Murphy came forth from the Strand Hotel, and after carefully slinging his long gray beard over his shoulder he cranked his car and warmed up the engine. He carefully removed the canvas covering from the musical mousetrap and ever so painstakingly arranged the spiral ramps and runways so that no mouse, no matter how careless, could stub a toe or bump a nose. He then climbed behind the steering wheel and the musical mouse-trap was underway!

A loud cheer arose from the crowd of children as Mr. Murphy yanked a lever and the reed organ started to play. Even before the cheering stopped the mice began to appear!

Through the streets of Centerburg rolled Mr. Michael Murphy and his musical mousetrap. The mice came running from every direction! Fat, doughnut-fed mice from Uncle Ulysses' lunchroom, thin mice from the churches, ordinary mice from the houses and homes, mice from the stores, and mice from the town hall.

They all went running up the ramps and runways, and disappeared in Michael Murphy's musical mousetrap. The children followed behind, enjoying the whole thing almost as much as the mice.

After traveling down every street in town, the procession came to a stop in front of the town hall, and the mayor came out and presented Mr. Murphy with his thirty-dollar fee—thirty bright, crisp, new one-dollar bills.

Just as the mayor finished counting out the bills into Mr. Murphy's hand, the sheriff stepped up and said, "Mr. Murphy, I hope this won't embarrass you too much, in fact I hate to mention it at all, but this

here micical moostrap, I mean mousetrap of yours, has got a license plate that is thirty years old . . . A *new* license will cost you just exactly thirty dollars."

Mr. Murphy blushed crimson under his beard. "It's the law, you know, and *I* can't help it!" apologized the sheriff.

Poor Mr. Murphy, poor *shy* Mr. Murphy! He handed his thirty dollars to the sheriff, took his new license plates and crept down the city hall steps. He climbed into his car and drove slowly away toward the edge of town, with the musical mouse-trap playing its reedy music. The children followed along to see Mr. Murphy release all of the mice.

"I really hated to do that, Mayor," said the sheriff as the procession turned out of sight on route 56A. "It's the law, you know, and if I hadn't reminded him he might have been arrested in the next town he visits." There's no telling how this demousing would have ended if the children's librarian hadn't come shouting "Sheriff! Sheriff! Quick! *We guessed the wrong book!*"

"What?" shouted the sheriff and the mayor and Uncle Ulysses.

"Yes!" gasped the children's librarian, "not *Rip Van Winkle*, but *another* book, *The Pied Piper of Hamelin!*"

"Geeminy Christmas!" yelled the sheriff, "and almost every child in town is followin' him this very minute!"

The sheriff and the librarian and the mayor and Uncle Ulysses all jumped into the sheriff's car and roared away after the procession. They met up with the children just outside the city limits. "Come back! Turn around, children!" they shouted.

"I'll treat everybody to a doughnut!" yelled Uncle Ulysses.

The children didn't seem to hear, and they kept right on following the musical mousetrap.

"The music must have affected their minds," cried the librarian.

"Sheriff, we can't lose all these children with election time coming up next month!" mourned the mayor. "Let's give Murphy another thirty dollars!"

"That's the idea," said Uncle Ulysses. "Drive up next to him, Sheriff, and I'll hand him the money."

The sheriff's car drew alongside the musical mousetrap, and Uncle Ulysses tossed a wad of thirty dollar bills onto the seat next to the shy Mr. Murphy.

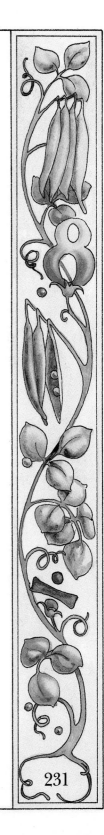

"Please don't take them away!" pleaded the librarian.

"Come, Murphy, let's be reasonable," shouted the mayor.

Mr. Murphy was very flustered, and his steering was distinctly wobbly.

Then the sheriff got riled and yelled at the top of his lungs, *"Get 'em low! Get 'em go! Durnit, Let 'em go!"*

And that's exactly what Mr. Murphy did. He let them go. He pulled a lever and every last mouse came tumbling out of the bottom of the musical mousetrap. And *such a sight* it was, well worth walking to the city limits to see. The mice came out in a torrent. The reedy organ on the musical mousetrap stopped playing, and the squeaking of mice and the cheering of children filled the air.

The torrent of mice paused, as if sensing direction, and then each Centerburg mouse started off in a straight, straight line to his own Centerburg mousehole. Mr. Murphy didn't pause. He stepped on

the gas, and the musical mousetrap swayed down the road. The mayor, the children's librarian, the sheriff, Uncle Ulysses, and the children watched as it grew smaller and smaller and finally disappeared.

Then Uncle Ulysses remembered the children. He turned around and noticed them grinning at each other and holding their thumbs in the air. They paid no attention whatever when they were called!

"That music has pixied these children!" he moaned.

"No, it hasn't, Uncle Ulysses," said Homer who had just come up. "There's not a thing the matter with them that Doc Pelly can't cure in two shakes! Just to be on the safe side, Freddy and I asked Doc

Pelly to come down to the school yard this morning
and put cotton in all the children's ears. You know,
just like Ulysses—not you, Uncle Ulysses, but the
ancient one, the one that Homer wrote about. Not
me, but the ancient one."

"You mean to say Doc Pelly is mixed up in this?"
asked the mayor.

"Yes, he thought it was awfully funny, our being
so cautious."

Uncle Ulysses laughed and said, "Round 'em up
and we'll all go down to the lunchroom for
doughnuts and milk."

"Sheriff," said the mayor, "with election time
coming next month *we* gotta put our heads together
and cook up a good excuse for spending sixty
dollars of the taxpayers' money."

The Dog in the Manger

from AESOP'S FABLES

retold by JOSEPH JACOBS

A dog looking out for its afternoon nap jumped into the manger of an ox and lay there upon the hay. But soon the ox, returning from its afternoon work, came up to the manger and wanted to eat some of the hay.

The dog, angry about being awakened from its nap, stood up and barked at the ox. Whenever the ox came near, hungry for the hay, the dog tried to bite it.

At last the ox said, "You do not eat hay. So there is no way you could enjoy eating my dinner yourself. Yet you will not let me eat it, though I am hungry and want it badly."

But the dog kept right on snapping and barking and growling. Finally the ox had to give up the hope of getting at the hay and went away, saying:

You should not begrudge to others
what you cannot enjoy yourself.

235

The Mouse's Tale

from

ALICE'S ADVENTURES IN WONDERLAND

by

LEWIS CARROLL

The mouse that Alice met in Wonderland was a storyteller and a poet. This mouse promised to tell Alice why he hated dogs as well as cats. And he did tell her a long story about a dog named Fury. But Alice's mind wandered between the mouse's tale and the mouse's tail. . . .

ine is a long and sad tale!" said the Mouse, turning to Alice, and sighing.

"It *is* a long tail, certainly," said Alice, looking down with wonder at the Mouse's tail. "But why do you call it sad?"

She kept on puzzling about it while the Mouse was speaking. So her idea of the tale was something like this.

"Fury said to
a mouse,
That he met
in the house,
'Let us both go
to law: *I* will
prosecute
you. Come, I'll
take no denial:
We must have
the trial; For
really this
morning I've
nothing to
do.' Said
the mouse
to the cur,
'Such a
trial,
dear sir,
with no
jury or
judge,
would
be wast-
ing our
breath.'
'I'll be
judge,
I'll be
jury,'
said
cun-
ning
old
Fury:
'I'll
try
the
whole
cause,
and
con-
demn
you to
death.'"

237

Jonathan Bing Does Arithmetic

by

BEATRICE CURTIS BROWN

When Jonathan Bing was young, they say,
He slipped his school and ran away,
Sat in the meadow and twiddled his thumbs
And never learned spelling or grammar or sums.

So now if you tell him, "Add one to two."
"Explain what you mean," he'll answer you.
"Do you mean 2-tomorrow or that's 2 bad?
And what sort of 1 do you want me to add?

"For there's 1 that was first when the race was 1
(For he ran 2 fast for the rest to run).
But if 2 had 1 when the race was through,
I'd say your answer was 1 by 2."

"Oh, Jonathan Bing, you haven't the trick
Of doing a sum in arithmetic."
"Oh, give me a chance, just one more try,"
Says Jonathan Bing with a tear in his eye.

"Very well, Jonathan, try once more,
Add up a hundred and seventy-four."
"A hundred and seventy-four," says he,
"Why—that's a great age for a person to be!"

239

The Magic Fishbone

by

CHARLES DICKENS

Once upon a time, long ago, there was a very fine king and a very lovely queen. They had sixteen children, and the oldest one was named Alicia.

One day Alicia's father, King Watkins the First, stopped by the market on his way home and bought a pound and a half of salmon for dinner. A cat followed him—not because he was king but because of the fish.

As he turned to shoo the cat away, he saw behind him a little old lady who was dressed in a long and lovely silk gown. She smelled of lavender, and she had the look of a worker-of-magic about her. She nodded to him, and he bowed low, certain that she was the Grand Marina.

"You are King Watkins the First, aren't you?" said the little old lady.

"I am," he answered, hoping that she would offer to grant him a wish. He was short of money, so he knew just what he would wish for—payday.

But the Grand Marina seemed to have something else on her mind. She glanced at the salmon he was carrying, and she said, "Tonight have Princess Alicia eat dinner with you and the queen. When she is finished with her helping of the salmon, she will find upon her plate. . . ." The lady paused.

"Yes, yes, what will my daughter find?" he asked.

"Don't interrupt!" she scolded. "You are just like all parents. You are too impatient. Princess Alicia will find a little fishbone. She should rub it and polish it until it shines like mother of pearl. Then, when she really needs help, if she wishes for the right thing at the right time, it will make her wish come true."

The king could hardly wait for dinnertime. Sure enough, when Princess Alicia finished her salmon, there was a little fishbone on her plate. Her father told her what the Grand Marina had said, so the princess rubbed the little fishbone and polished it until it shined like mother of pearl. Then she put it in her pocket to use when she really needed help to make a wish come true.

The next morning, after King Watkins the First left for work, the queen got sick to her stomach. She felt much too bad to fix breakfast for her children, and the cook had quit last week because the royal family did not have enough money to pay her.

"Whatever shall we do?" sighed the queen.

Princess Alicia said, "Don't worry, Mama. I can take care of everything."

The queen wondered if Alicia would pull out her magic fishbone. But Alicia just pulled out the pots and pans and went to work. She made porridge for all the little princes and princesses, and she gave two tablespoons of awful-tasting medicine to her mother.

The queen was feeling a bit better by the time the king came home that evening. But she was still lying down with a headache.

King Watkins the First helped Alicia get all of the younger children ready for bed. Then he watched her as she put cold cloths on the queen's forehead.

"My dear daughter," he started.

"Yes, Papa," said Alicia.

"Where is the magic fishbone?"

"In my pocket, Papa," said Alicia.

"You haven't forgotten, have you, that it can make a wish come true?" asked King Watkins.

"Oh, no, Papa," said Alicia. "I mean to use it when I need to."

The next day was a hot summer day, but rainy, so all the little princes and princesses had to play inside. The baby fell into the fireplace and got a lump on his head and a black eye and a mouthful of ashes. So he cried and roared and yelled at the top of his voice.

No nurse came running, because King Watkins the First did not have enough money to pay a nurse to take care of his children. But Princess Alicia came running.

She picked up the baby and made sure that he had not broken any bones. She washed his face and held a cold cloth on the lump on his head. Then Princess Alicia said, "Stick out your tongue, dear." And she wiped the ashes out of the baby's mouth. Soon he was nodding off to sleep in her arms.

She was still rocking the baby when her father came in.

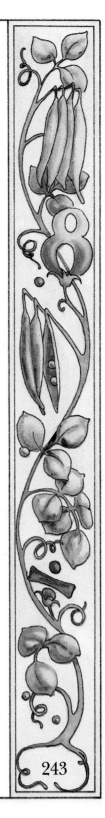

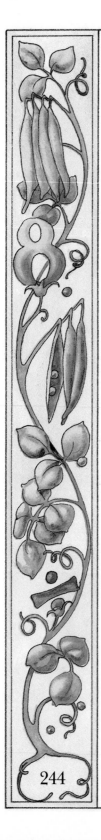

All the other little princes and princesses told him what had happened.

He looked at Alicia. "My dear daughter," he started.

"Yes, Papa," said Alicia.

"Where is the magic fishbone?"

"In my pocket, Papa," said Alicia.

"You haven't forgotten, have you, that it can make a wish come true?" asked King Watkins.

"Oh, no, Papa," said Alicia. "I mean to use it when I need to."

As she put the baby down, she told all the other little princes and princesses to bring her their clothes that needed washing. When she had finished doing the wash and hanging their things up to dry, she came back to her father.

He was holding his head and sighing sadly.

"What is the matter, Papa?" asked Princess Alicia.

"My dear daughter, I have no money, and payday is still more than a week away."

"Isn't there some way for you to get the money you need before payday?" she asked.

"I have tried my best," said King Watkins the First. "But I can't find a way."

"Well," said Princess Alicia. "When we have tried our best, and that is not enough, then it is time to ask

for help." She reached in her pocket for the magic
fishbone. "I wish for payday," she said.

Suddenly it was payday! Gold coins came rattling
down the chimney. They covered the floor. But that
was not all.

Up came the Grand Marina riding in a coach
pulled by eight peacocks. She waved her fan, and
away flew Princess Alicia's apron. Suddenly she was
wearing a beautiful dress.

Then the Grand Marina tapped each little prince
and princess on the head with her fan. As she did,
one after another appeared in new clothes from top
to toes. She even tapped King Watkins the First and
the queen, and suddenly they were in fine royal
robes.

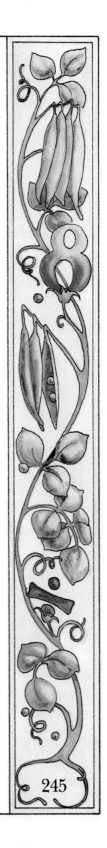

"Now that you're all dressed up, I suppose you're ready for a party," said the Grand Marina. So she gave a wonderful party, with cakes and cookies that covered all the tables. When everyone was stuffed, she announced, "From now on, there will be an extra payday every month of the year!"

Then King Watkins the First jumped up and said, "Hooray!"

The Grand Marina smiled at Princess Alicia. "This is what comes," she said, "of waiting until you really need help, and then making the right wish at the right time."

A·C·K·N·O·W·L·E·D·G·M·E·N·T·S

Acknowledgment is gratefully made to the following individuals and publishers for permission to reprint these selections.

"The Lama." From *Verses From 1929 On* by Ogden Nash. © 1931 by Ogden Nash. © renewed 1985 by Frances Nash, Isabel Nash Eberstadt, and Linnell Nash Smith. Reprinted by permission of Little, Brown and Company.

"One Guess." From *The Poetry of Robert Frost,* edited by Edward Connery Lathem. © 1923, 1969 by Holt, Rinehart and Winston, Inc. © 1936, 1951 by Robert Frost. © 1964 by Lesley Frost Ballantine. Reprinted by permission of Henry Holt and Company, Inc.

"Ben and Me." From *Ben and Me* by Robert Lawson. © 1939 by Robert Lawson, © renewed 1967 by John W. Boyd. Reprinted by permission of Little, Brown and Company.

"I Watched an Eagle Soar." © 1989 by Virginia Driving Hawk Sneve. Reprinted from *Dancing Teepees: Poems of American Indian Youth* by permission of Holiday House.

While the selection appears as originally written, selected words have been replaced to accommodate reading level; obscure references have been clarified; and longer selections have been slightly abbreviated. The following selections have adjusted vocabulary: "The Glorious Whitewasher" by Mark Twain, "Amy's Trouble at School" by Louisa May Alcott, "Robinson Crusoe on the Island" by Daniel Defoe, "Ben and Me" by Robert Lawson, "Two Big Bears" by Laura Ingalls Wilder, "Rip Van Winkle" by Washington Irving, and "The Magic Fishbone" by Charles Dickens.

I·L·L·U·S·T·R·A·T·I·O·N C·R·E·D·I·T·S

Acknowledgment is gratefully made to the following for permission to reprint these illustrations.

PAGE   ILLUSTRATOR

10   Pamela R. Levy. © 1991 by Jamestown Publishers, Inc. All rights reserved.

15   Norman Rockwell.

18   Jessie Willcox Smith. Reprinted by permission of P. S. P. Licensing Corporation.

23   Frank T. Merrill.

25–27   Thomas Ewing Malloy. © 1991 by Jamestown Publishers, Inc. All rights reserved.

28–29, 32–36   Anonymous.

30–31   Howard Pyle. Courtesy of the Delaware Art Museum, Wilmington. Howard Pyle Collection.

161   Michael Hague. From *The Lion, the Witch and the Wardrobe* by C. S. Lewis, illustrated by Michael Hague. Illustrations © 1981 by Macmillan Publishing Company. Reprinted by permission of Macmillan Publishing Company.

165, 169, 171   Pamela R. Levy. © 1991 by Jamestown Publishers, Inc. All rights reserved.

175   Trina Schart Hyman. From *Greedy Mariani and Other Folktales of the Antilles,* illustrated by Trina Schart Hyman. Illustrations © 1974 by Atheneum Publishers. Reprinted by permission of Margaret K. McElderry Books, an imprint of Macmillan Publishing Company.

177   Pamela R. Levy. © 1991 by Jamestown Publishers, Inc. All rights reserved.

178–179   Edward Lear.

180   Timothy C. Jones. © by Timothy C. Jones.

181   Trina Schart Hyman. Illustration © 1988 by Trina Schart Hyman. Reprinted by permission of Scholastic Inc.

183, 186   Bob Eggleton. © 1991 by Jamestown Publishers, Inc. All rights reserved.

189   Alfred de Breanski. Courtesy of Art Licensing International, Inc.

190, 195, 199, 204   N. C. Wyeth.